LARGE PRINT
DOT-to-DOT

LARGE PRINT
DOT-to-DOT

CREATE AMAZING VISUAL PUZZLES

THUNDER BAY
P·R·E·S·S
San Diego, California

Thunder Bay Press
An imprint of Printers Row Publishing Group
10350 Barnes Canyon Road, Suite 100, San Diego, CA 92121
www.thunderbaybooks.com

Printers Row Publishing Group is a division of Readerlink Distribution Services, LLC.
Thunder Bay Press is a registered trademark of Readerlink Distribution Services, LLC.

All notations of errors or omissions should be addressed to Thunder Bay Press, Editorial Department,
10350 Barnes Canyon Road, Suite 100, San Diego CA 92121. All other correspondence (author inquiries,
permissions) concerning the content of this book should be addressed to Arcturus Holdings Limited,
26/27 Bickels Yard, 151-153 Bermondsey Street, London SE1 3HA, info@arcturuspublishing.com

Thunder Bay Press
Publisher: Peter Norton
Publishing team: Ana Parker, Kathryn Chipinka, Aaron Guzman
Editorial team: JoAnn Padgett, Melinda Allman, Traci Douglas

ISBN: 978-1-68412-096-3
CH005855NT
Supplier 29, Date 0717, Print run 6508

Printed in China

21 20 19 18 17 2 3 4 5 6

INTRODUCTION

You will find that each of these puzzles is very different. Some are simple and soothing, and you can enjoy the meditative experience of smoothly rolling your pen across the page from one dot to the next. Other puzzles require some patience, featuring more stylized illustrations where consecutive numbers are often spaced far apart and part of the puzzle is locating the next dot. Each puzzle should be approached in a different way, although we recommend using a ruler to draw your lines for all of the puzzles.

The larger print size also means that these puzzles can be enjoyed by a wider range of readers, whose eyesight may be diminished. The dots and numbers are more visible compared to what you may find in other puzzle books, making the whole process less taxing for the eyes.

Each image contains between 150 and 200 dots, and the subjects range from flowers, animals, everyday scenes and objects to landscapes, spiritual symbols, and zodiac constellations. With so many varied illustrations to uncover, there is something here for everyone.

So pick up your pen or pencil and get ready to join the dots!

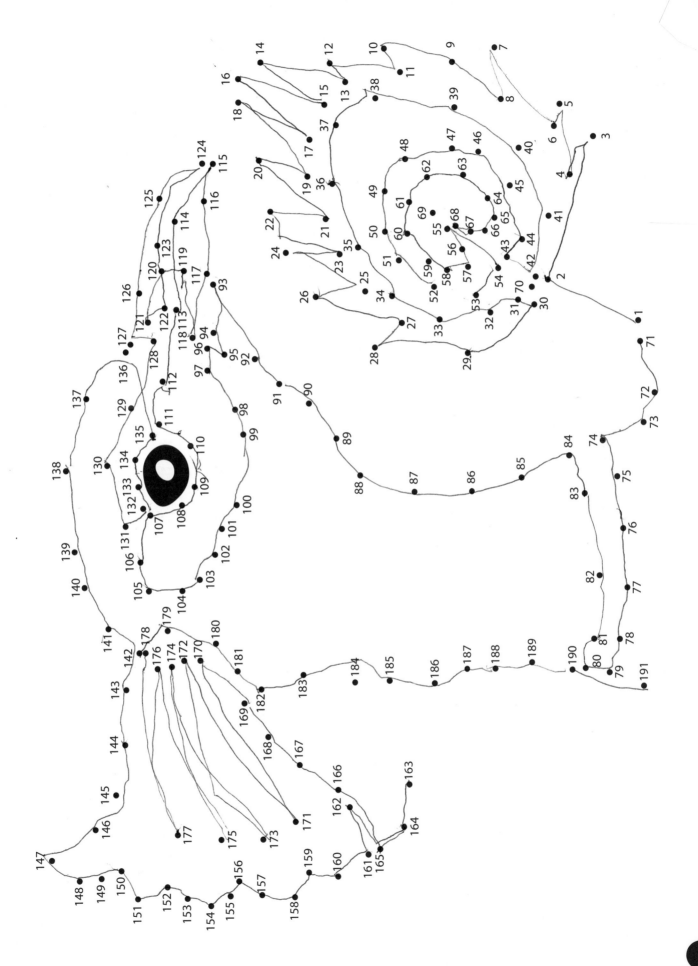

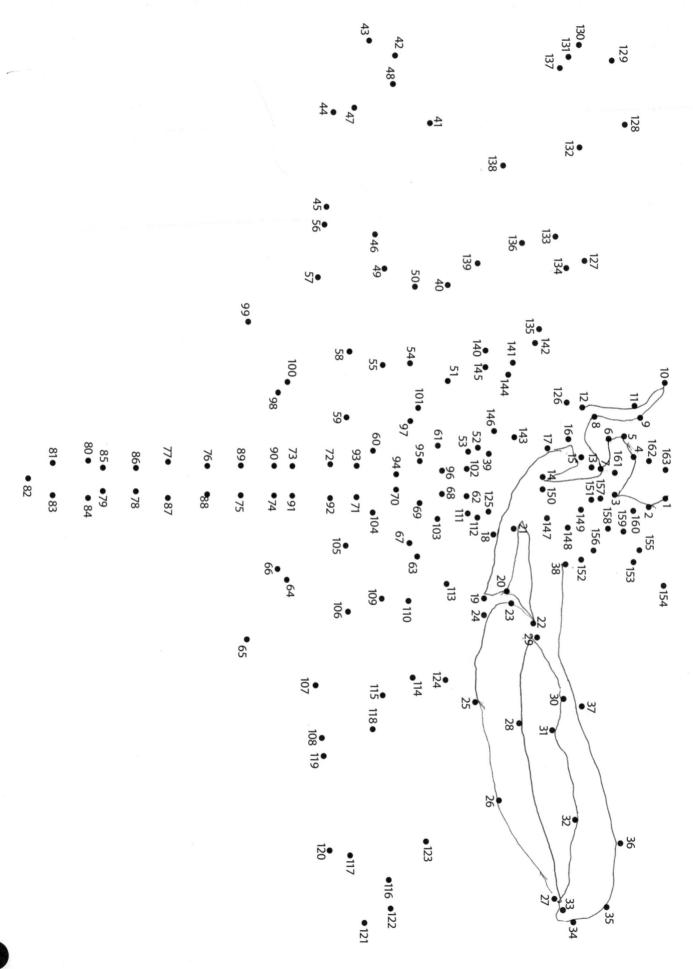

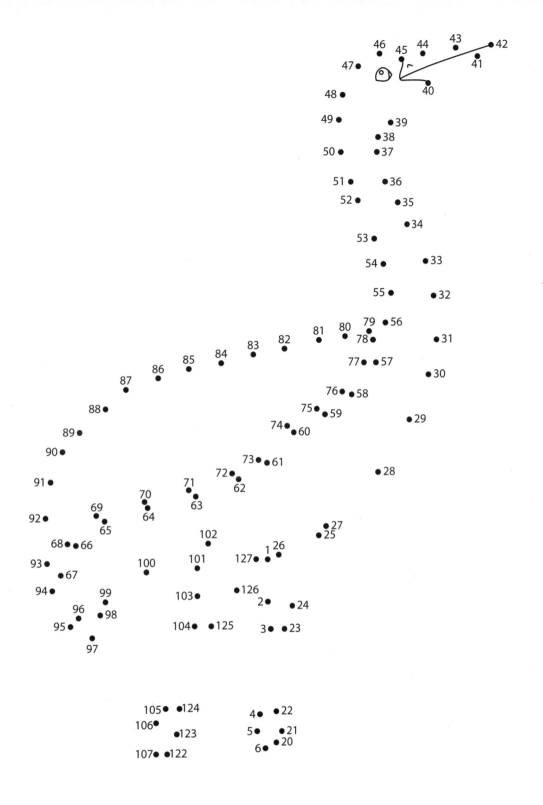

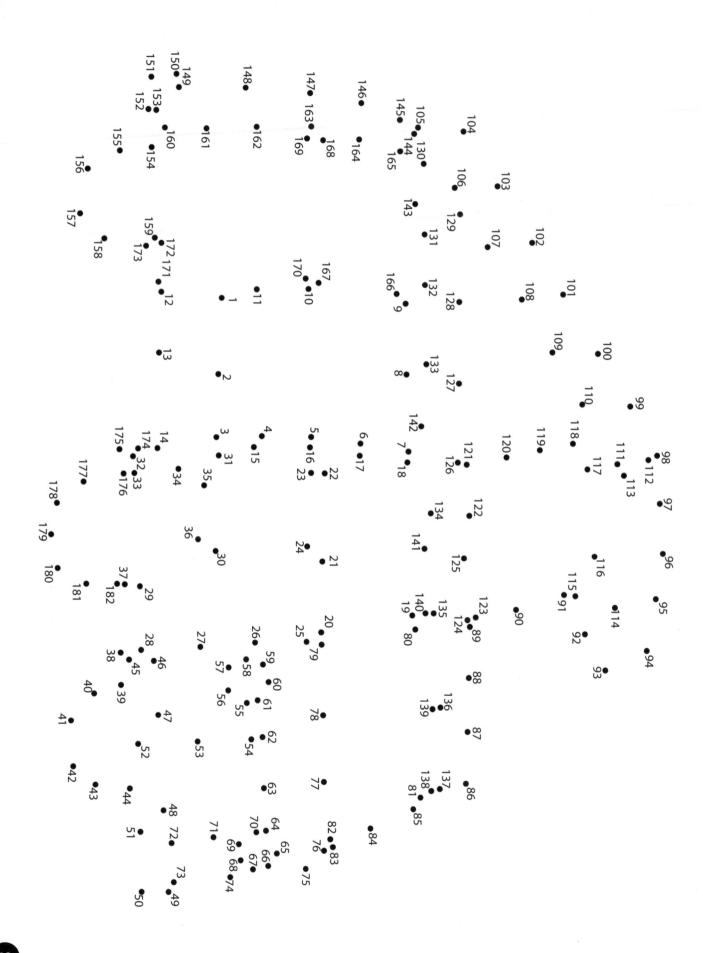

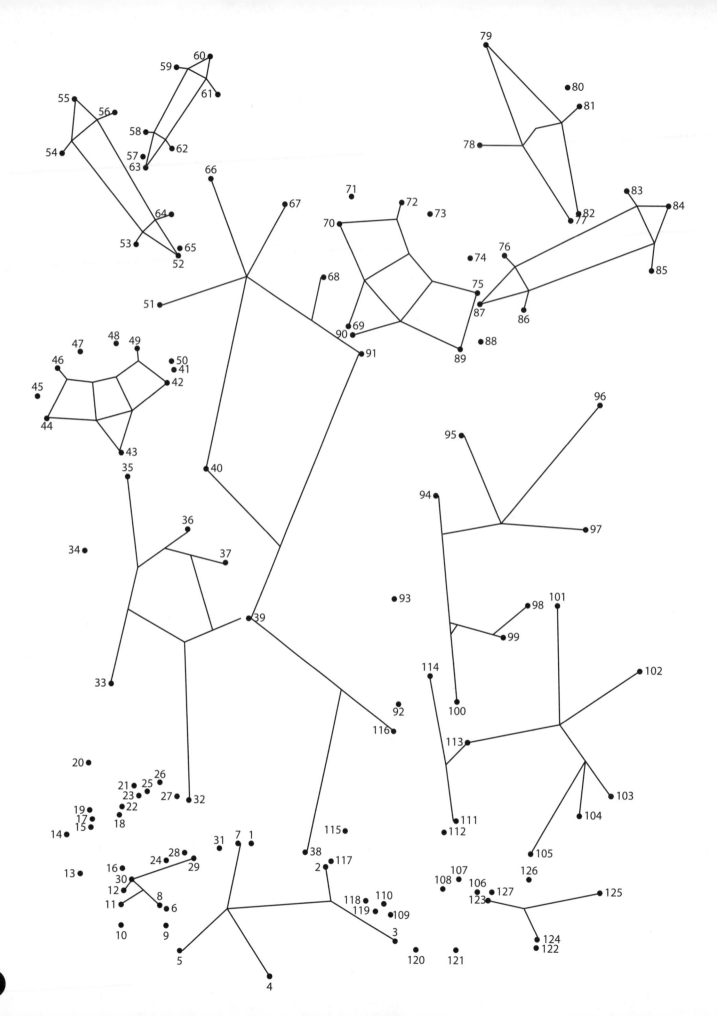

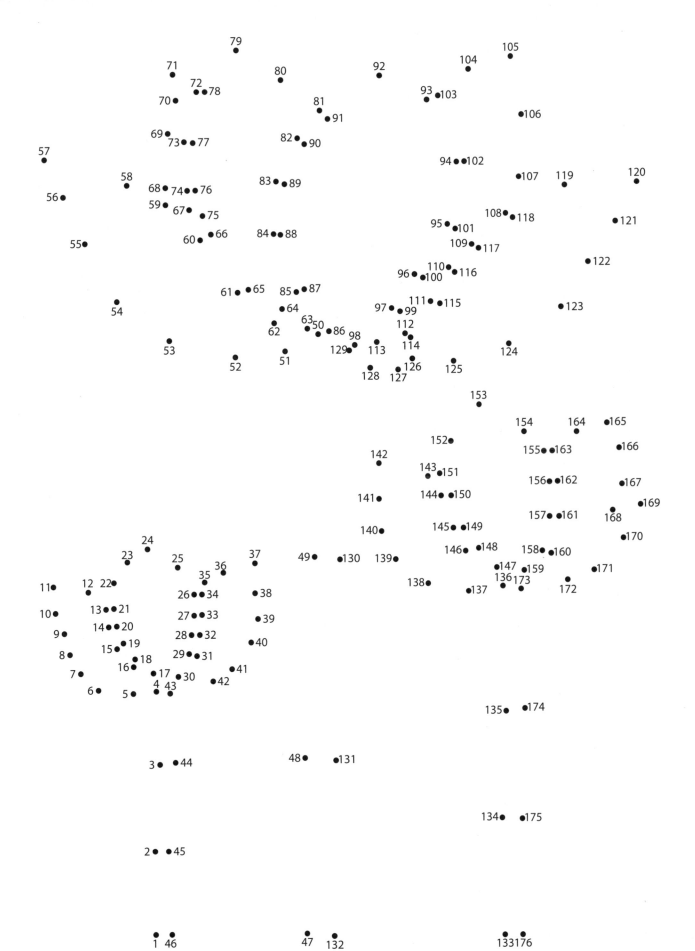

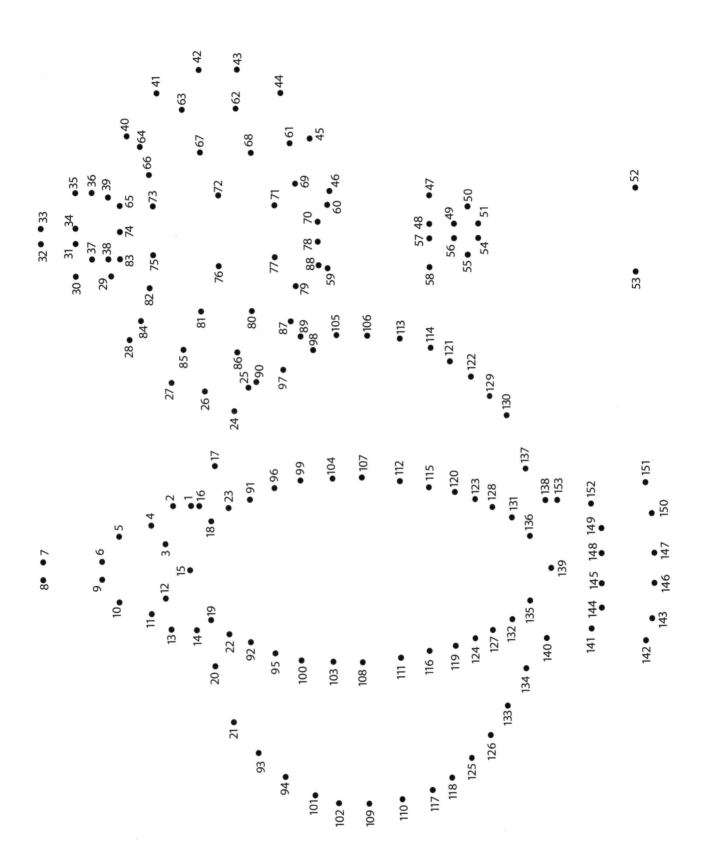

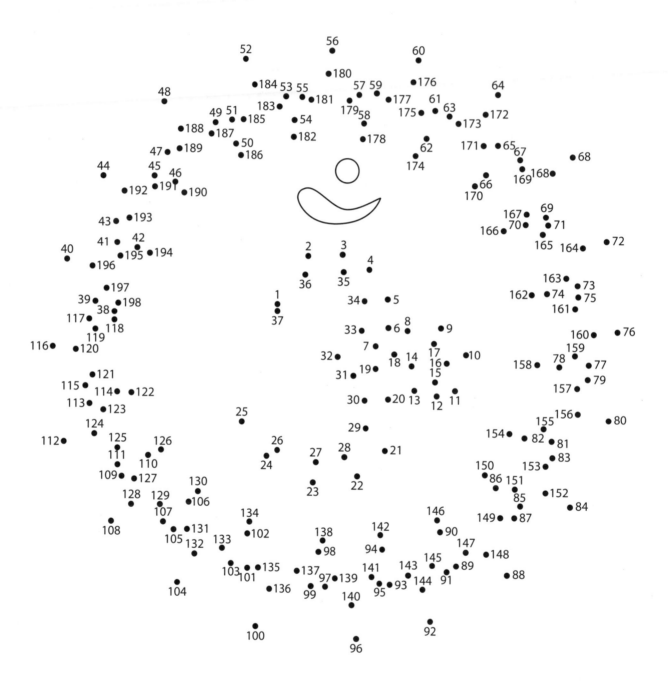

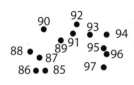
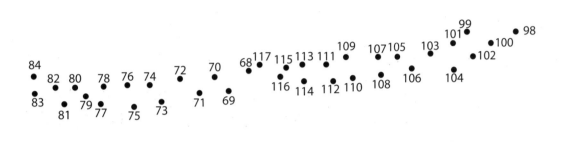
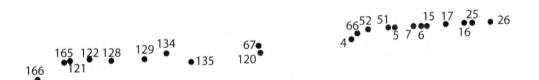

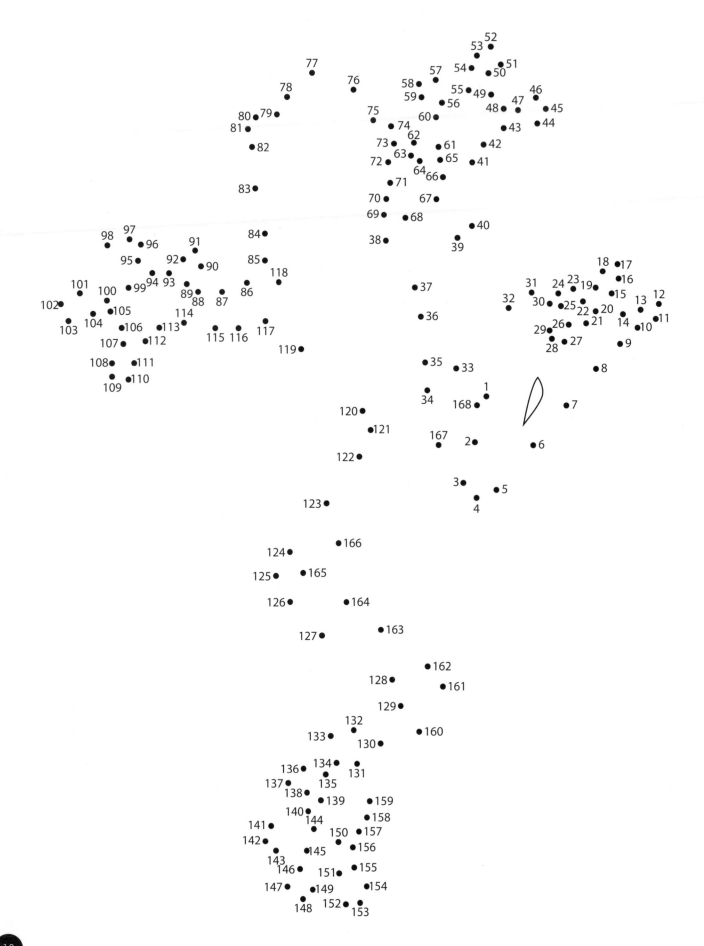

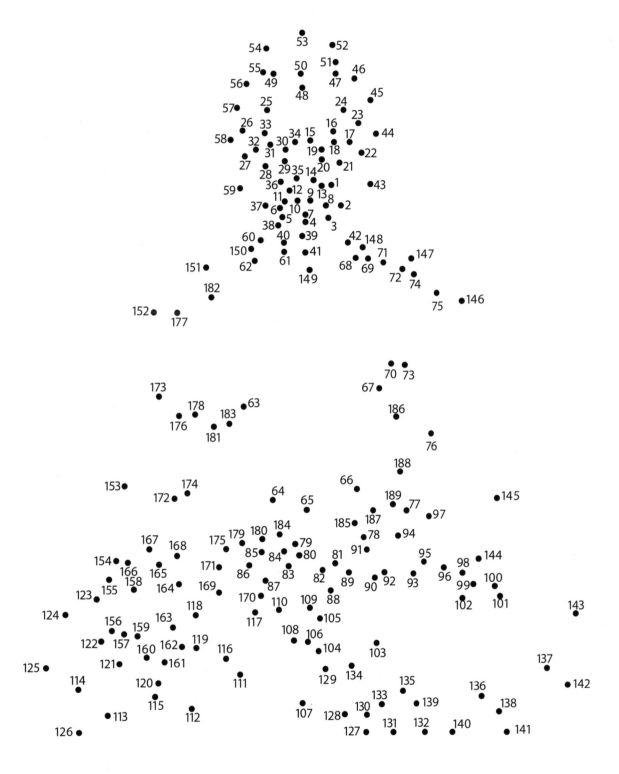

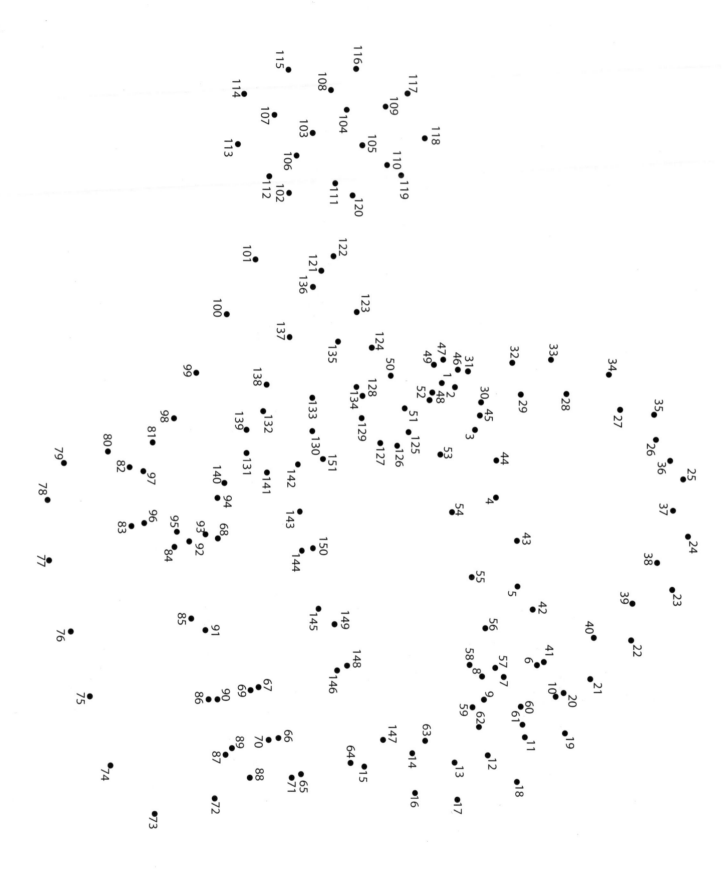

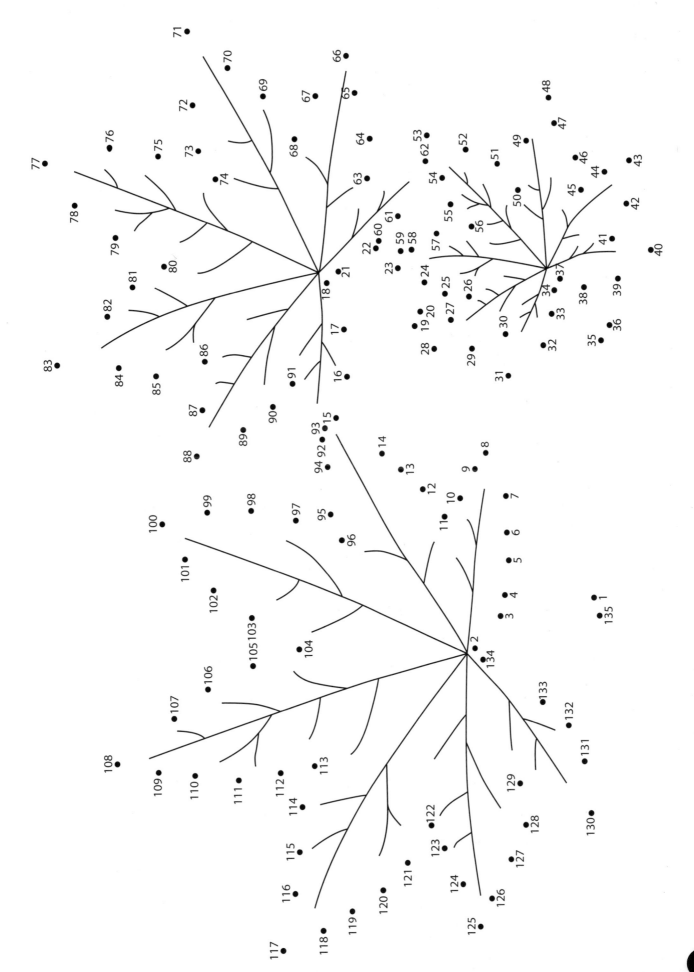

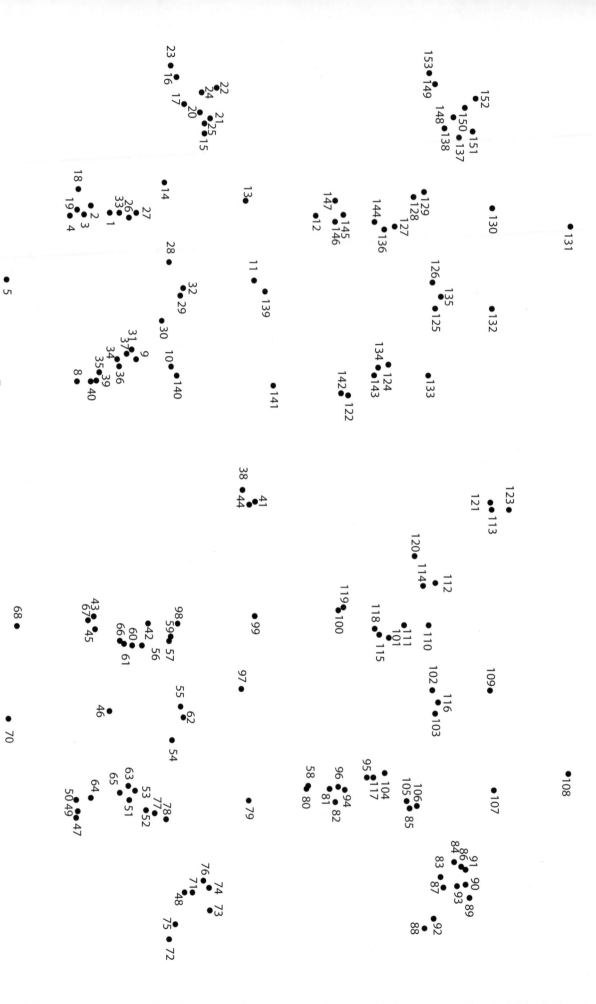

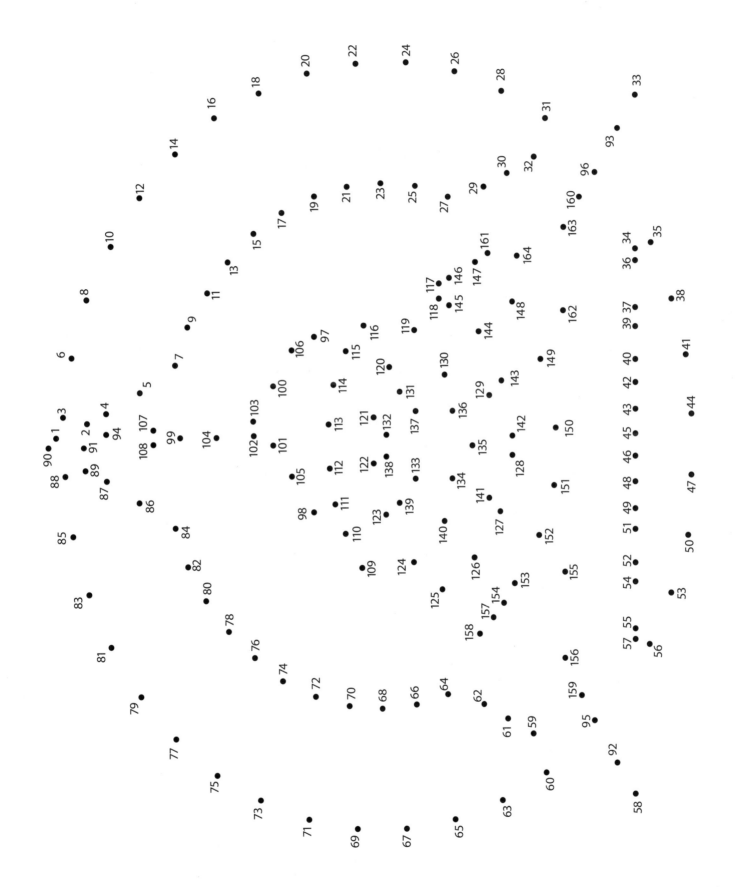

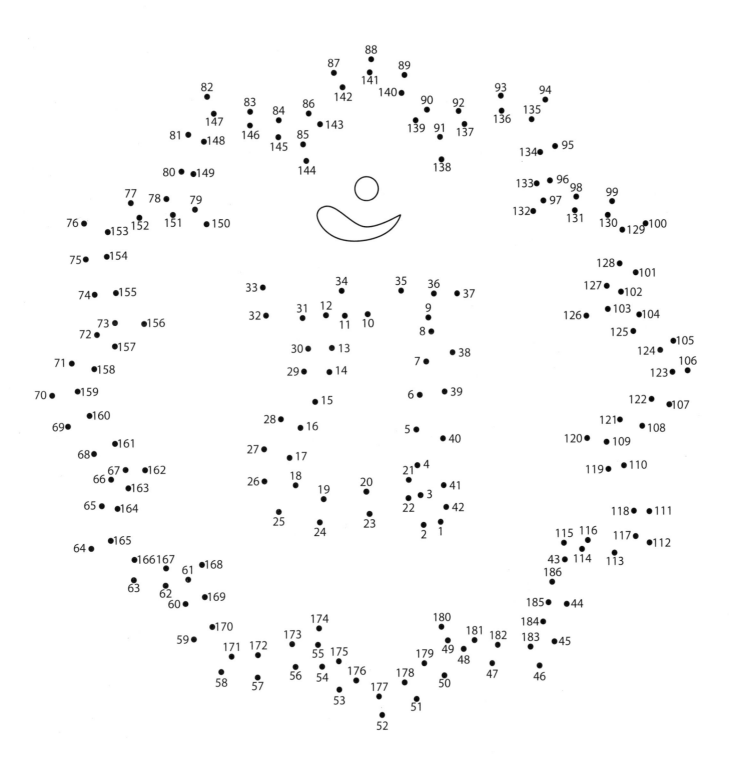

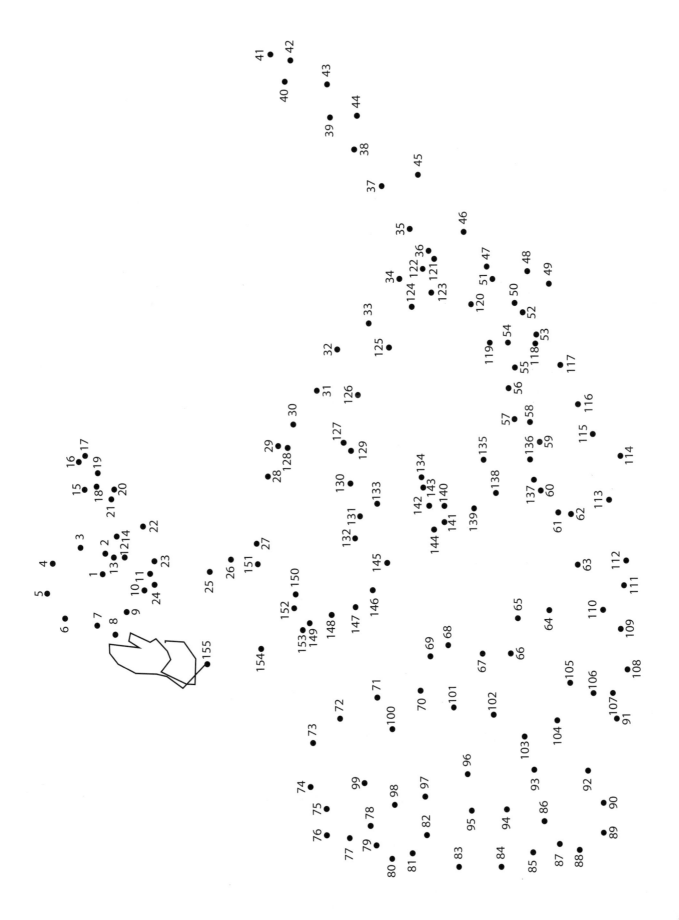

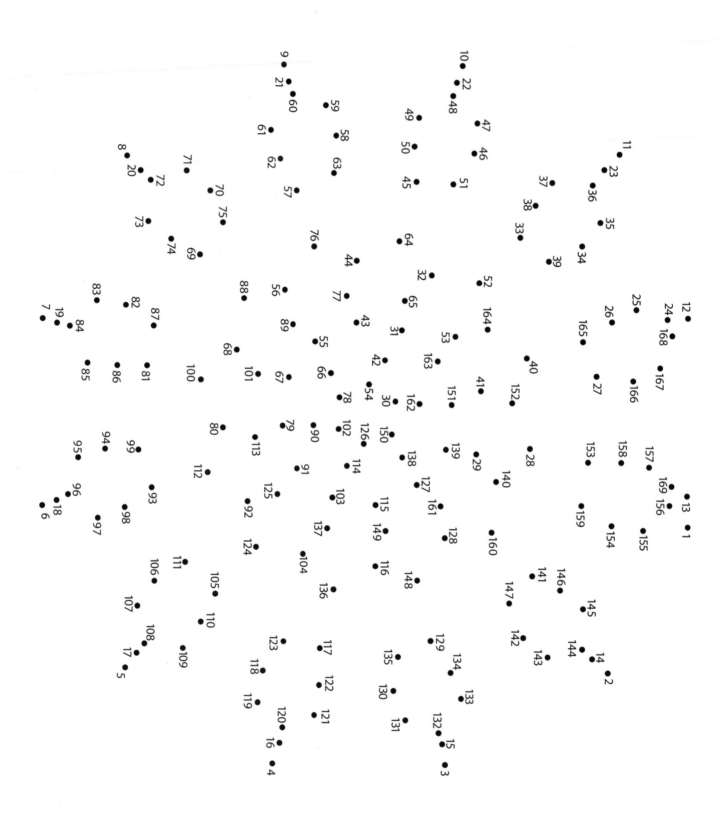

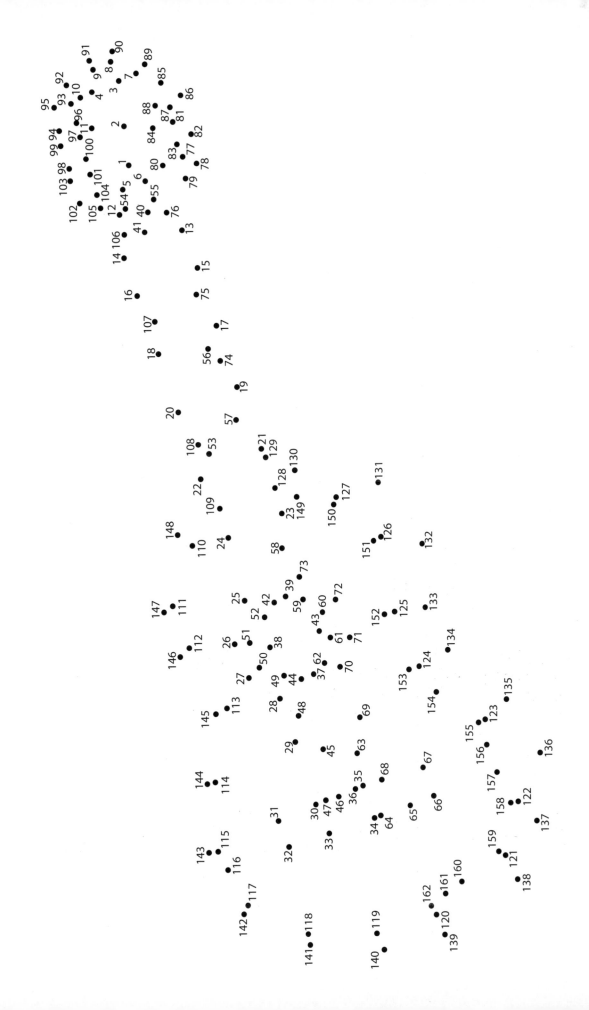

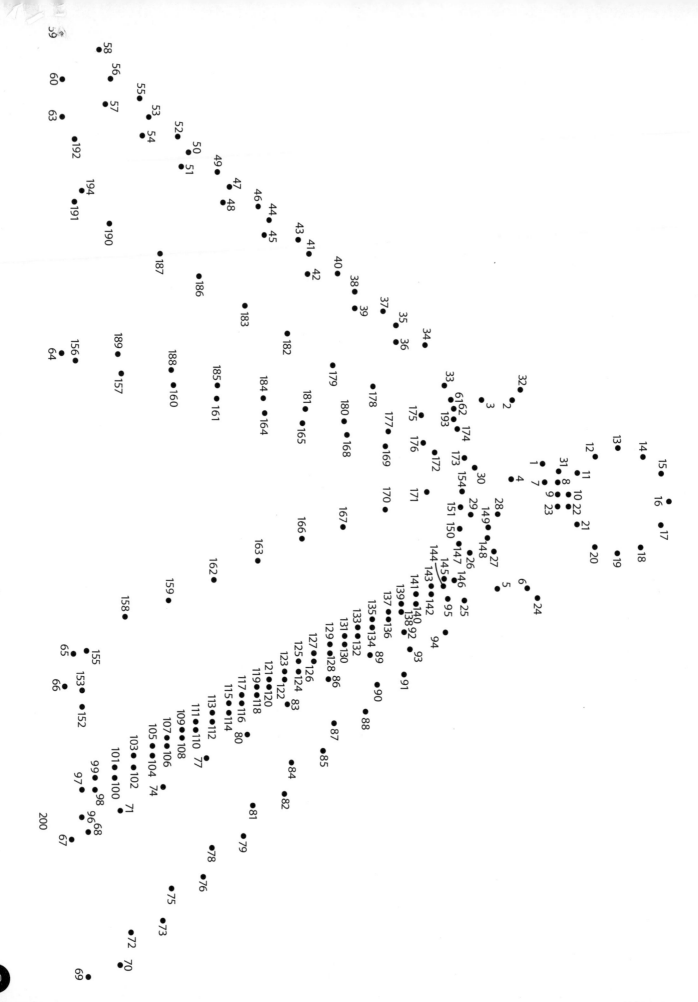

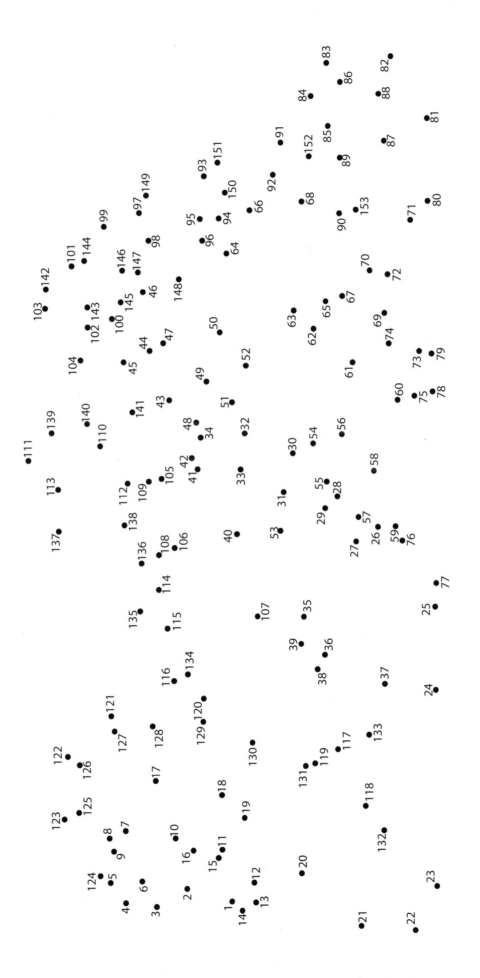

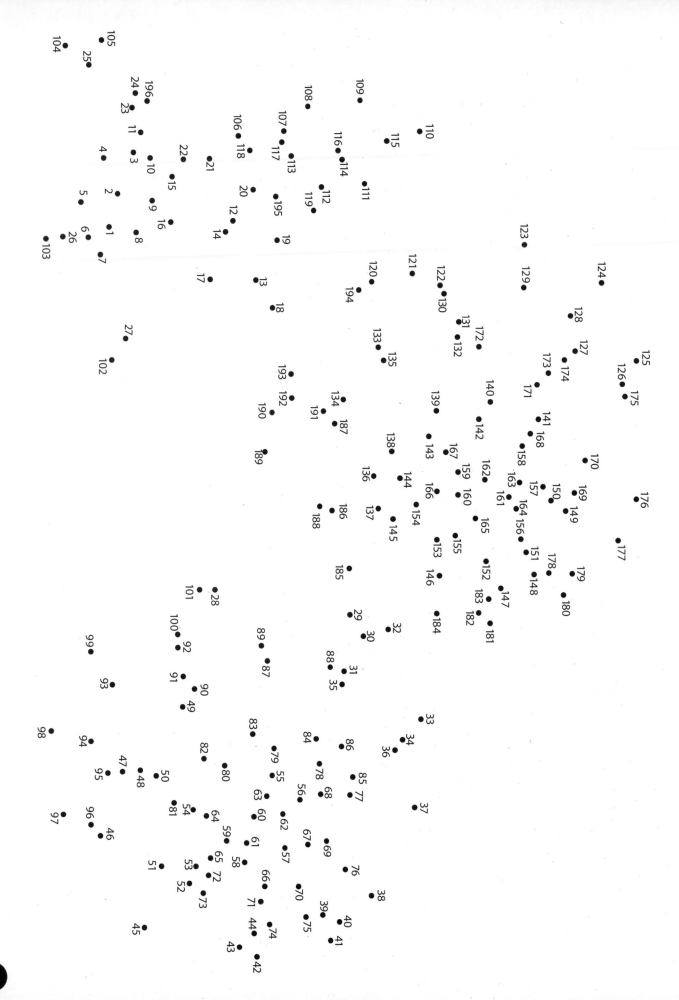

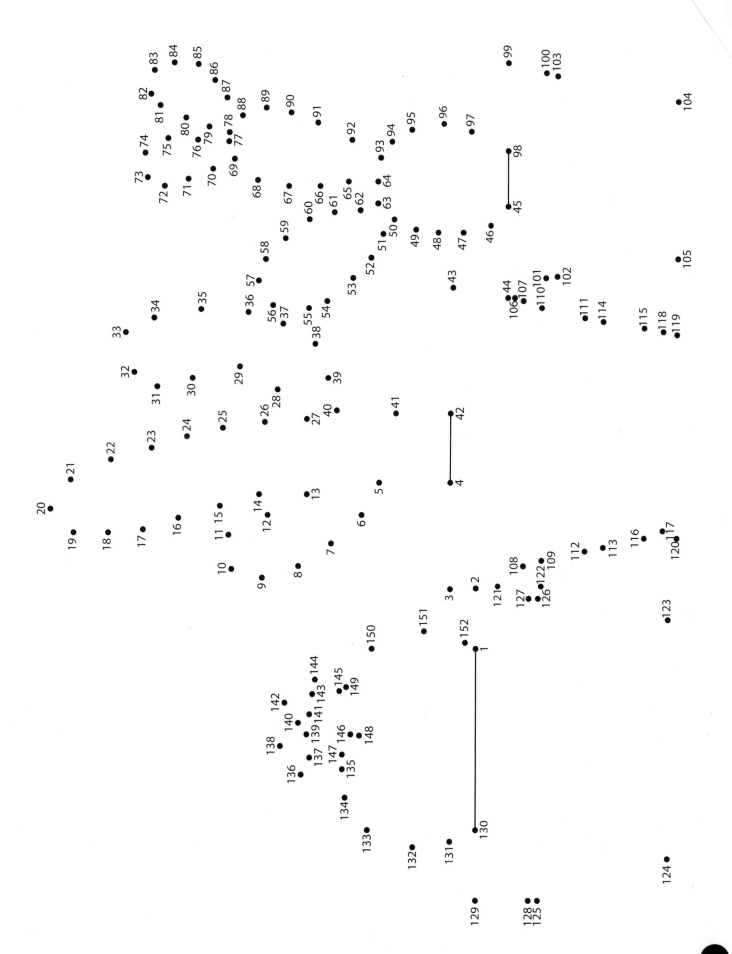

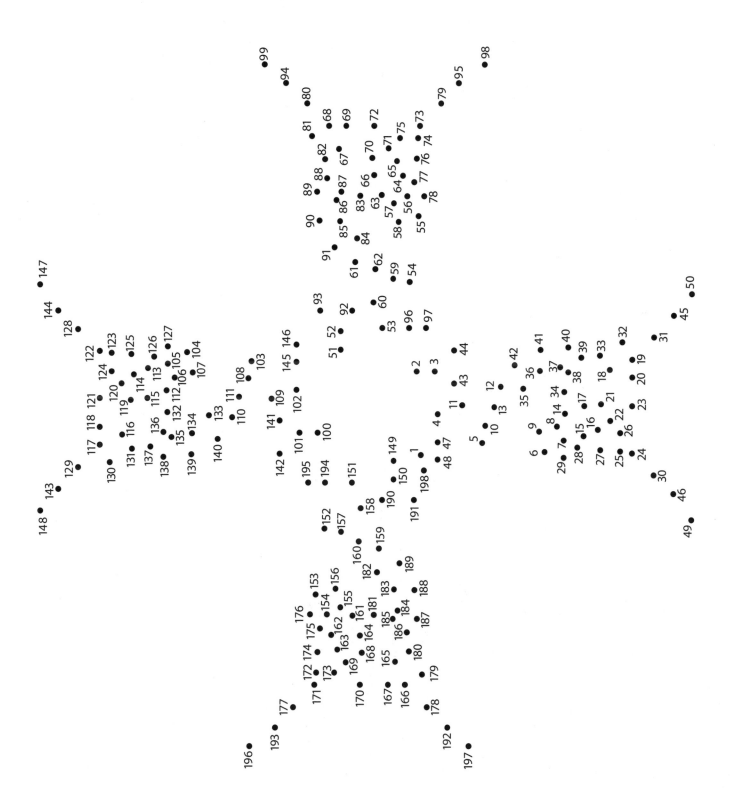

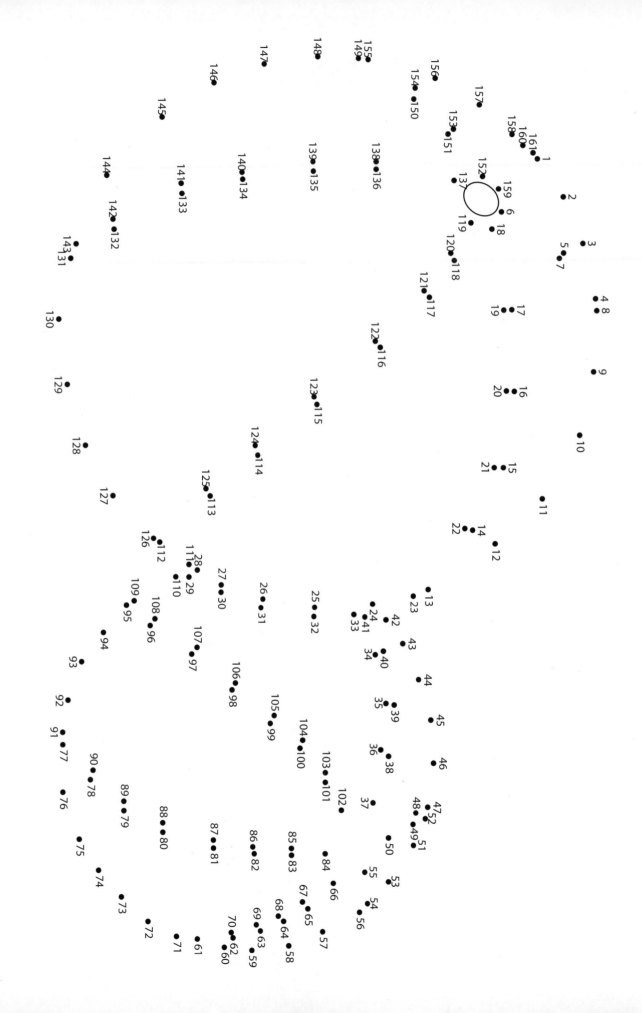

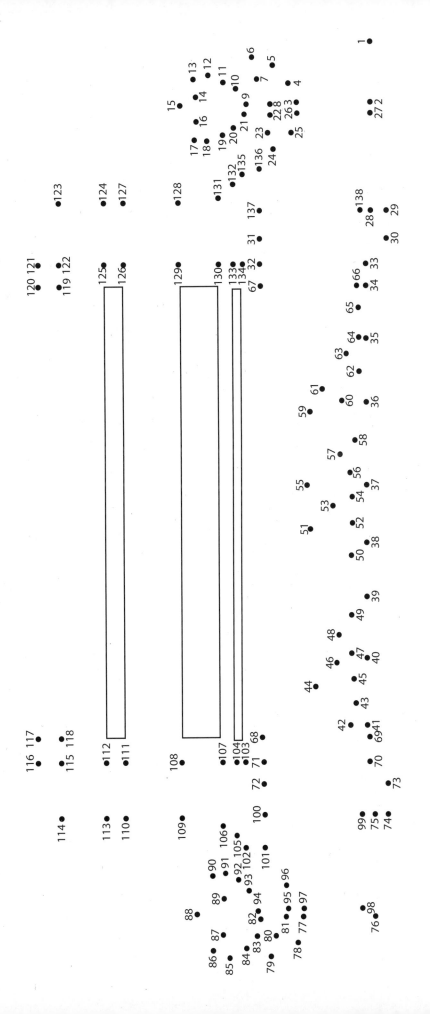

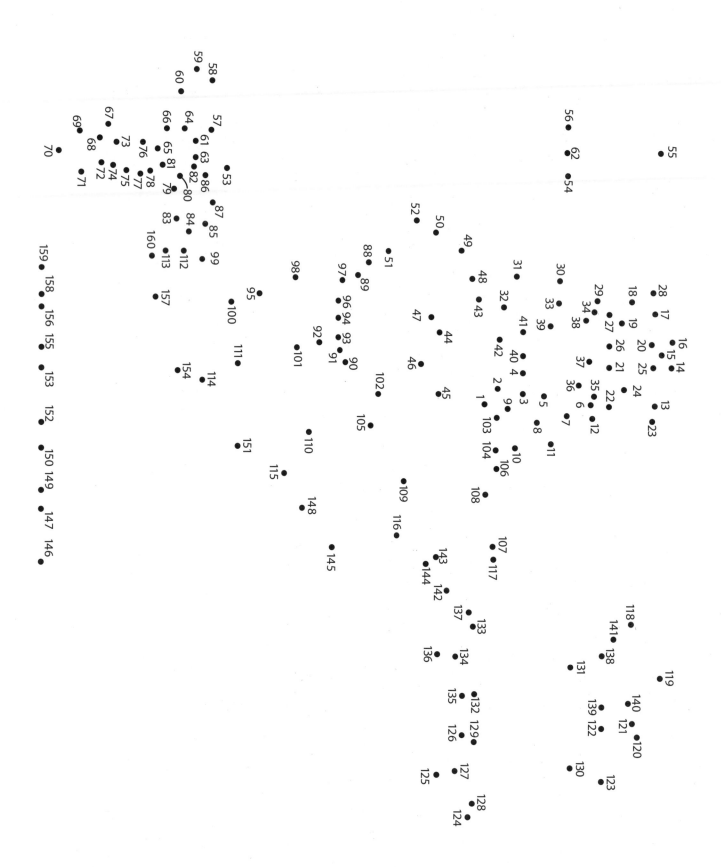

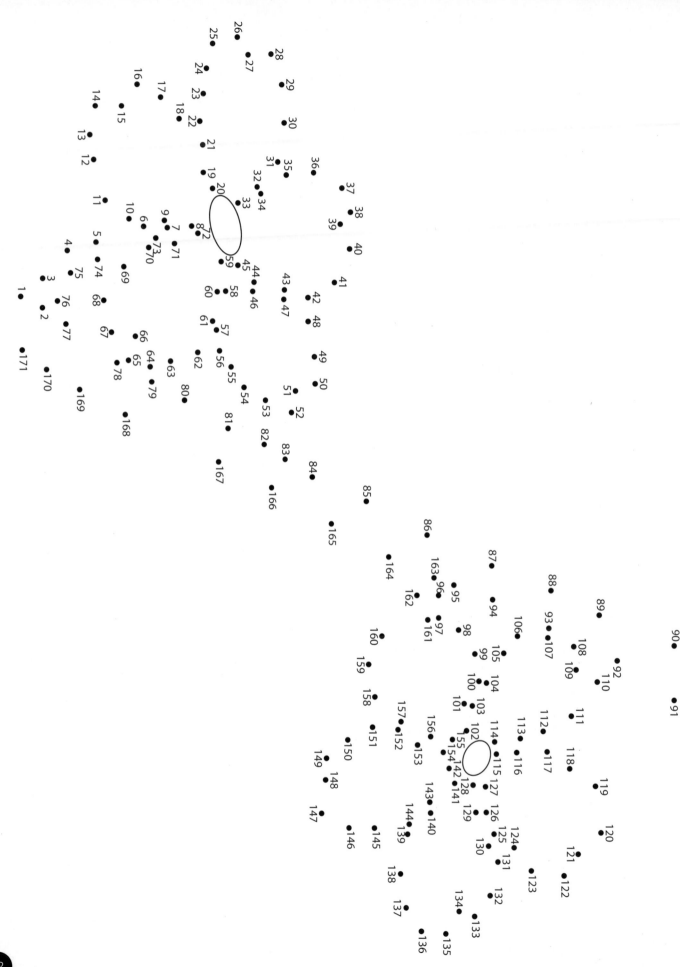

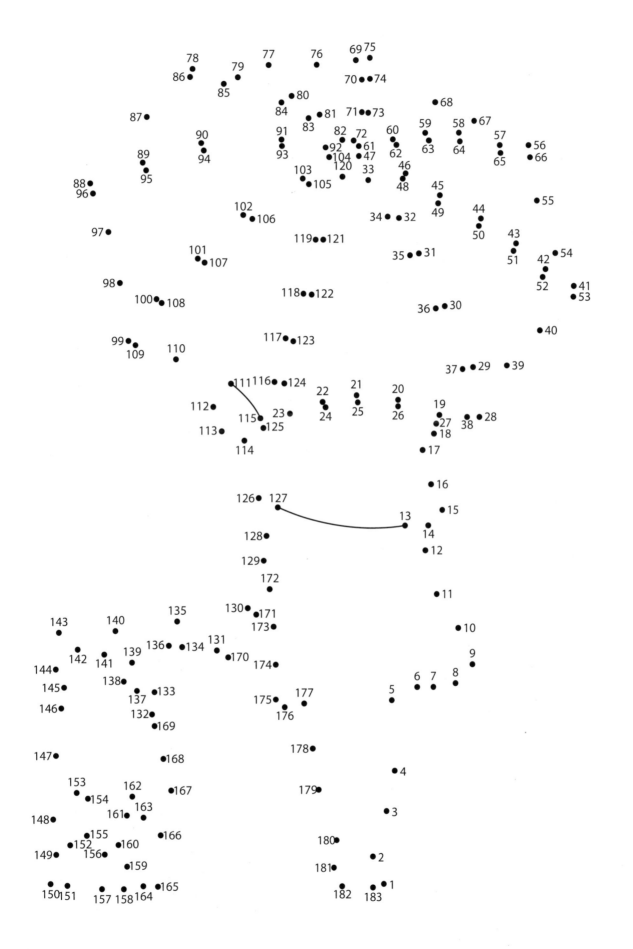

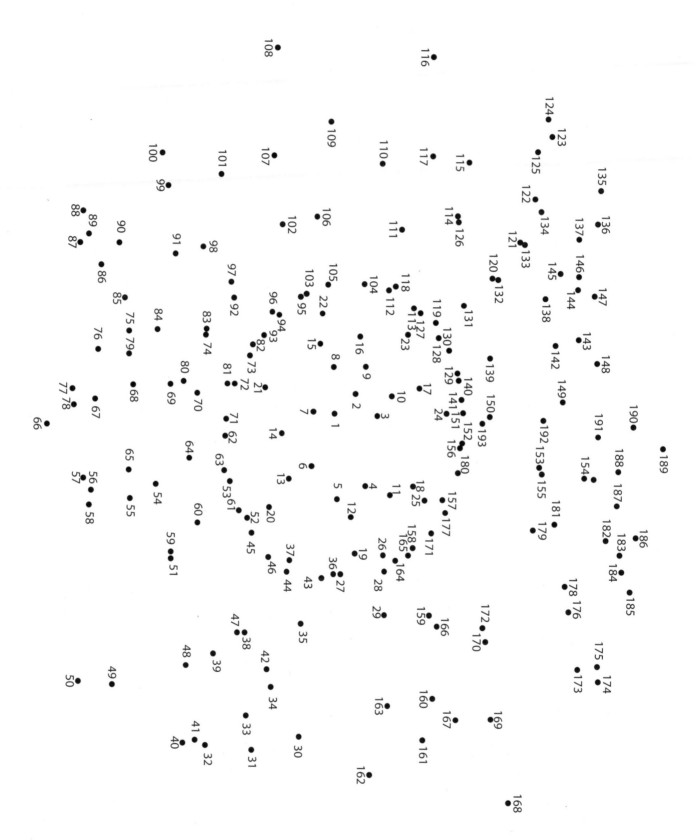

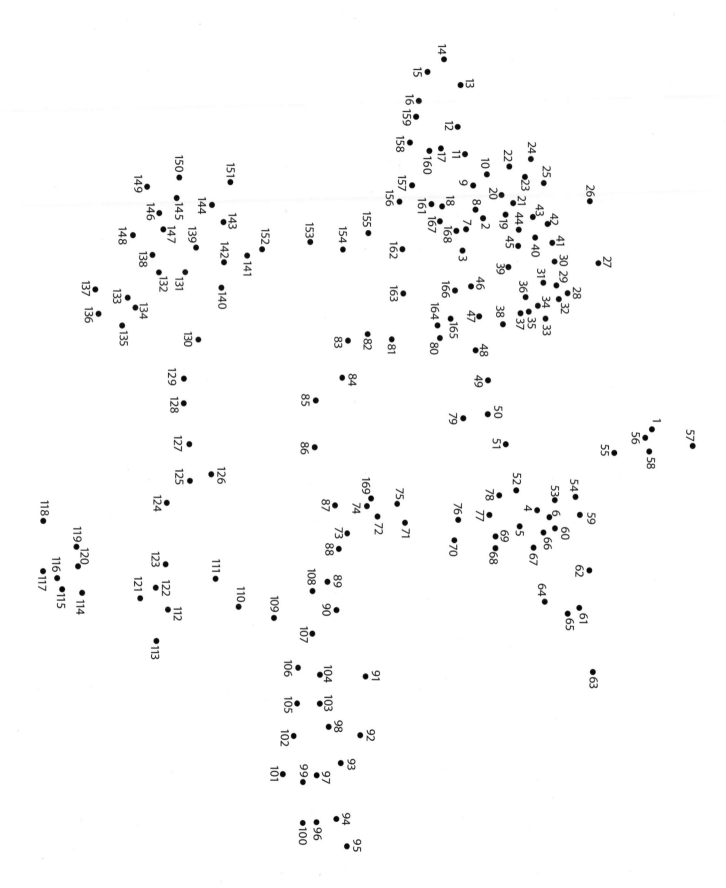

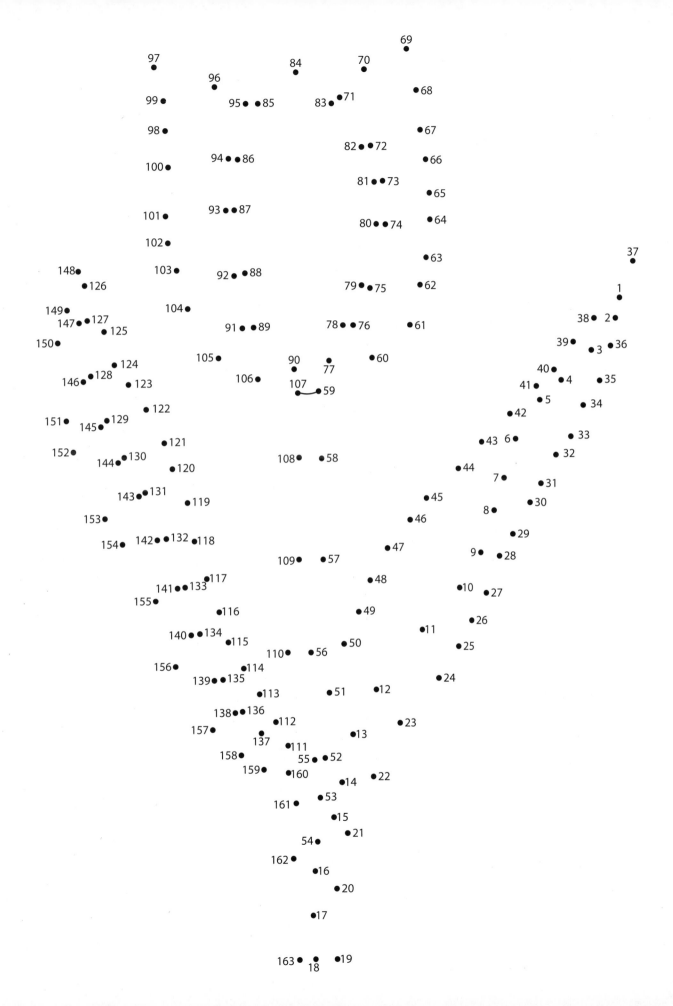

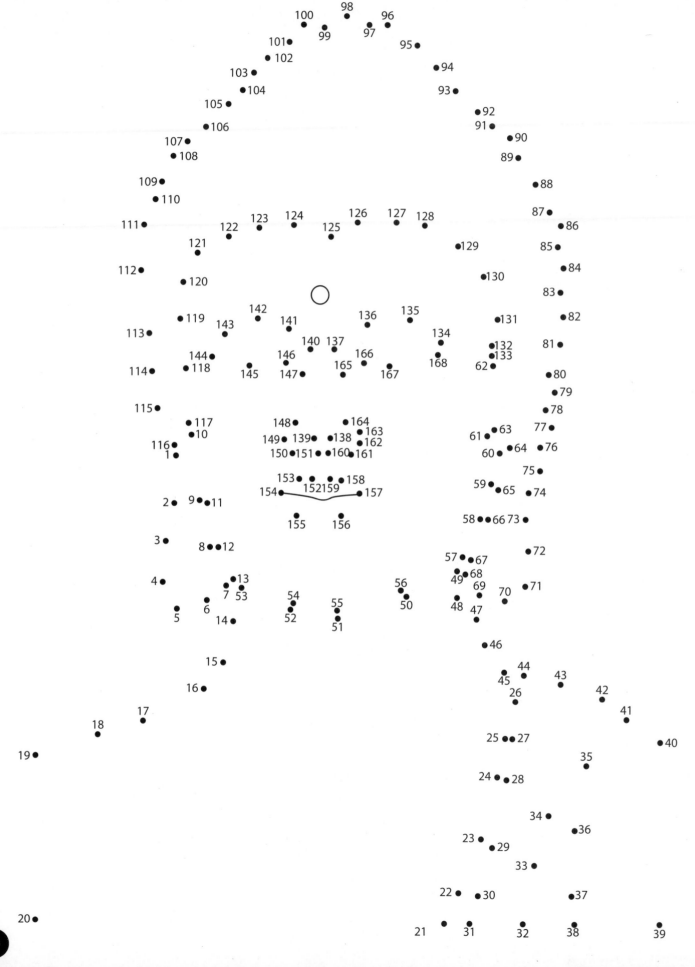

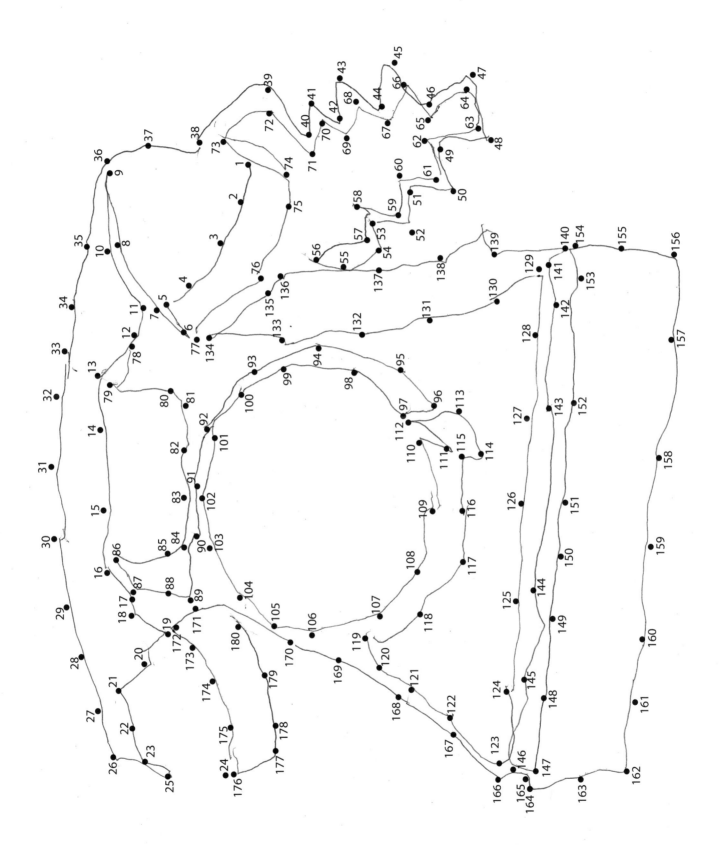

49

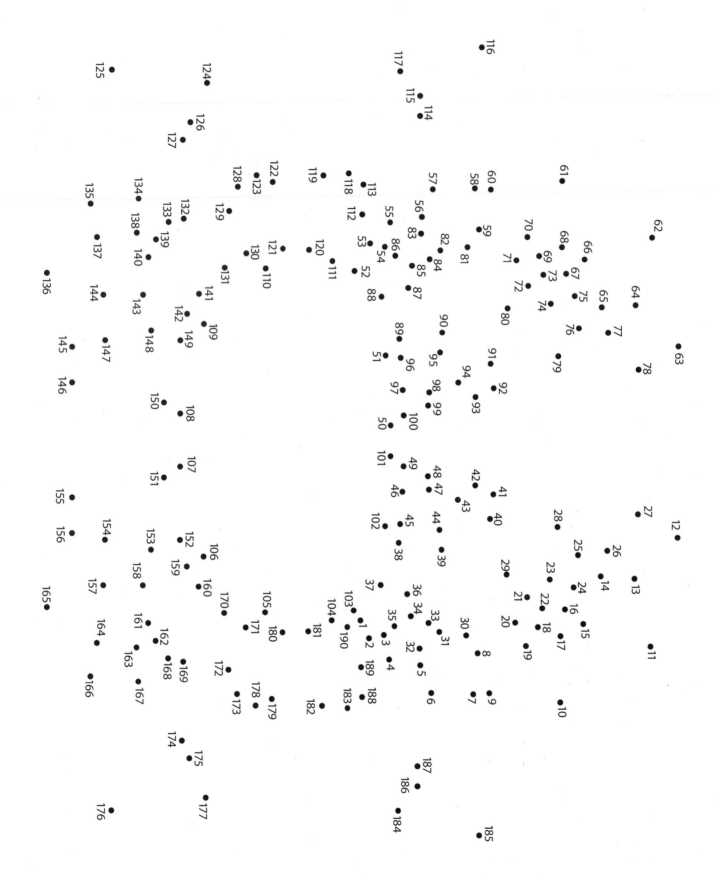

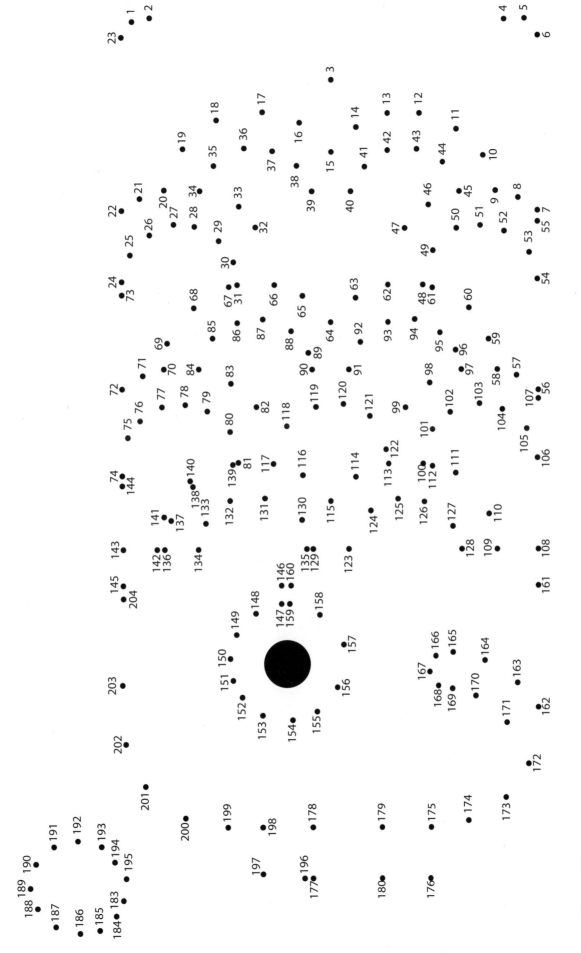

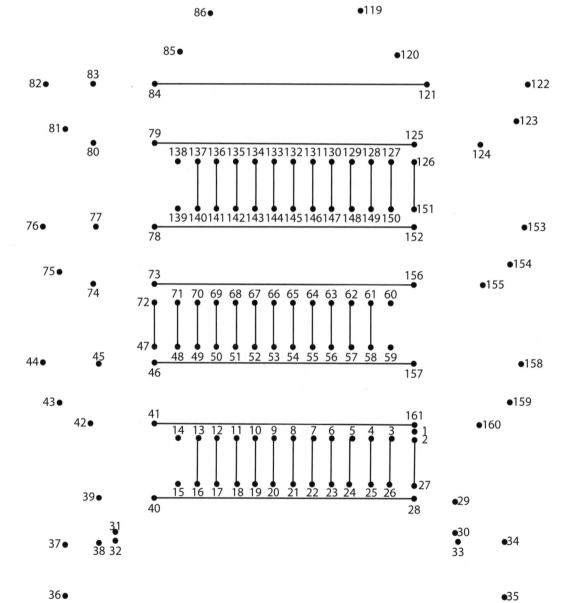

53

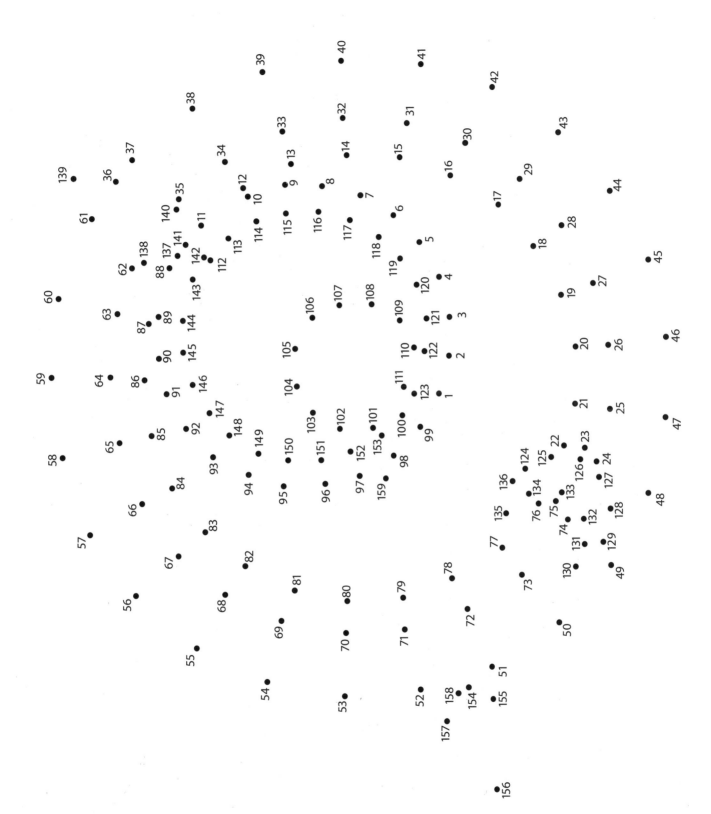

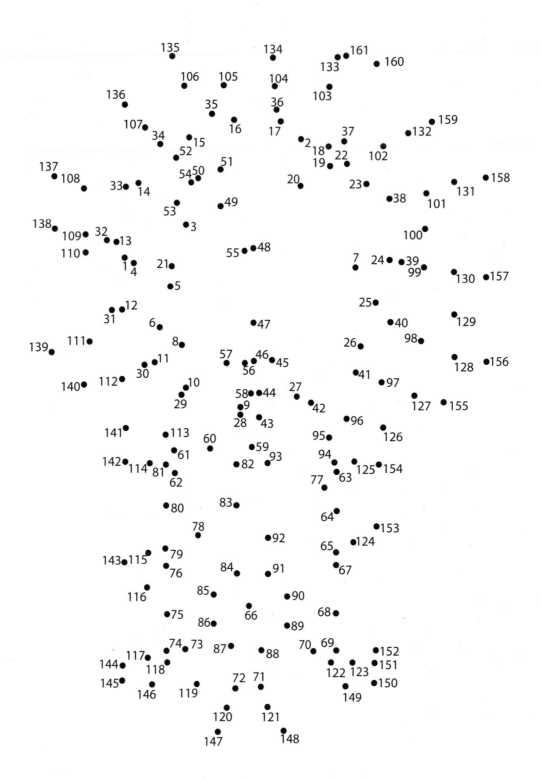

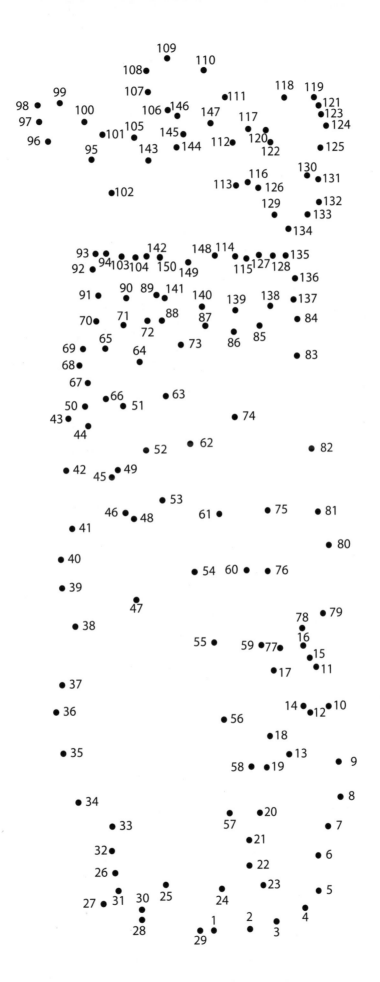

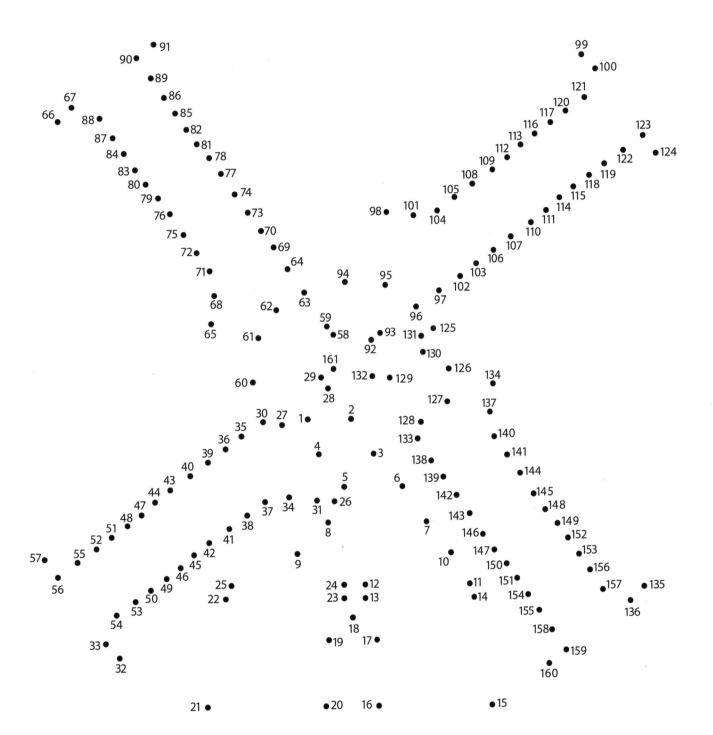

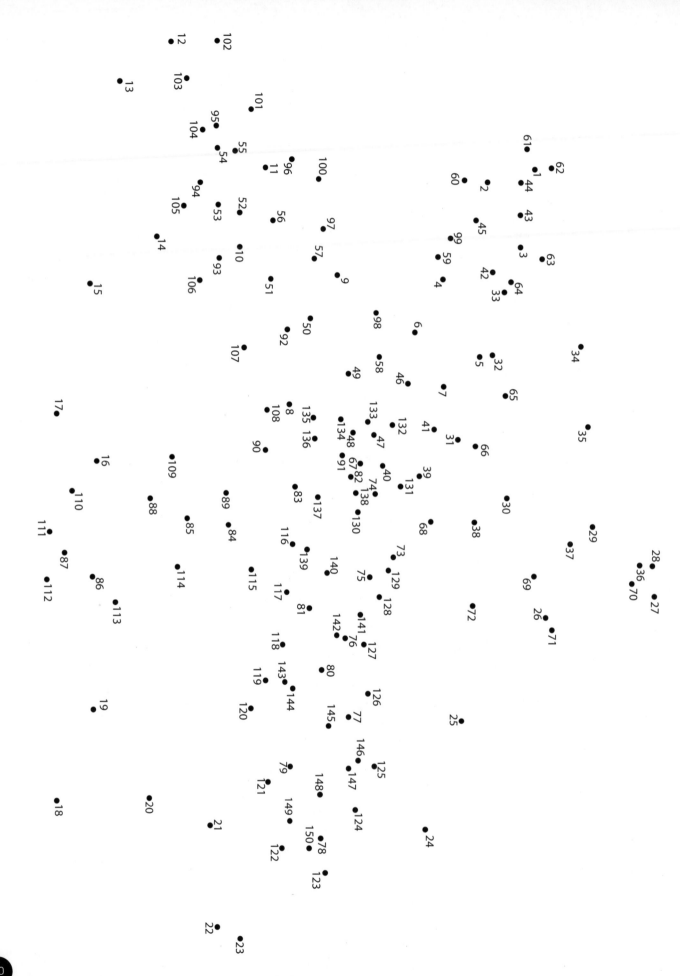

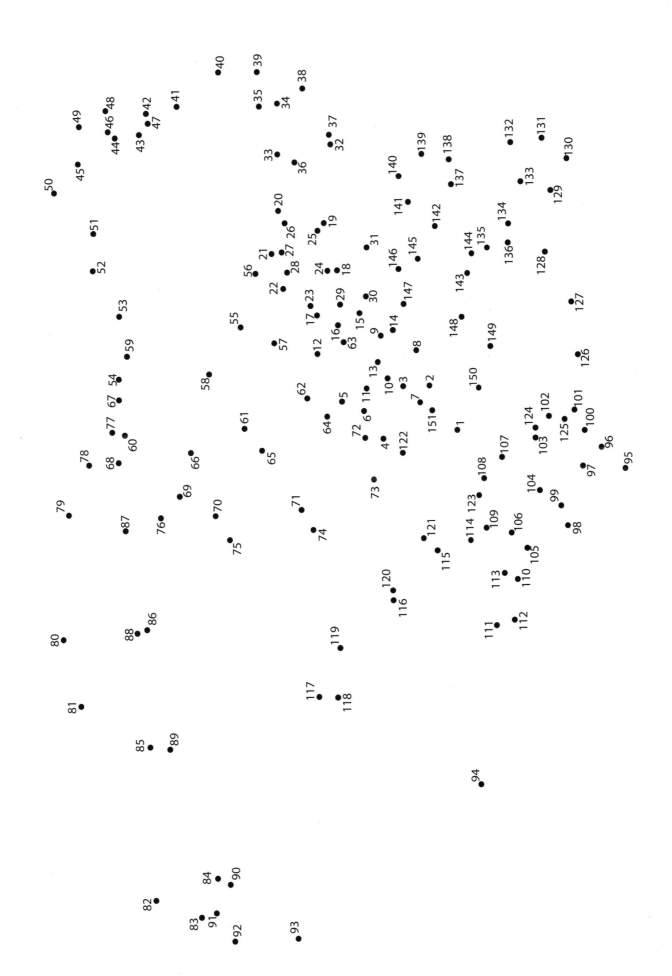

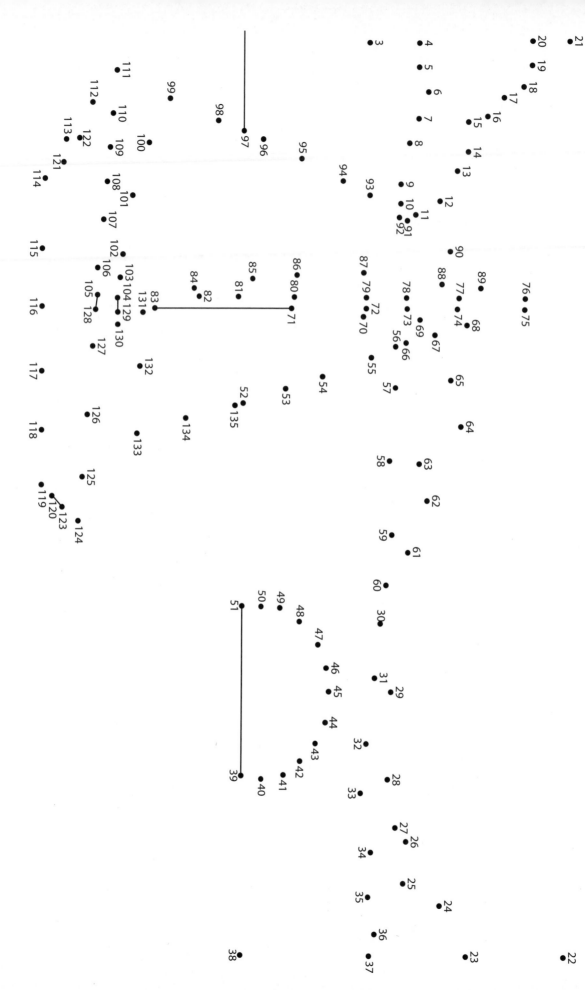

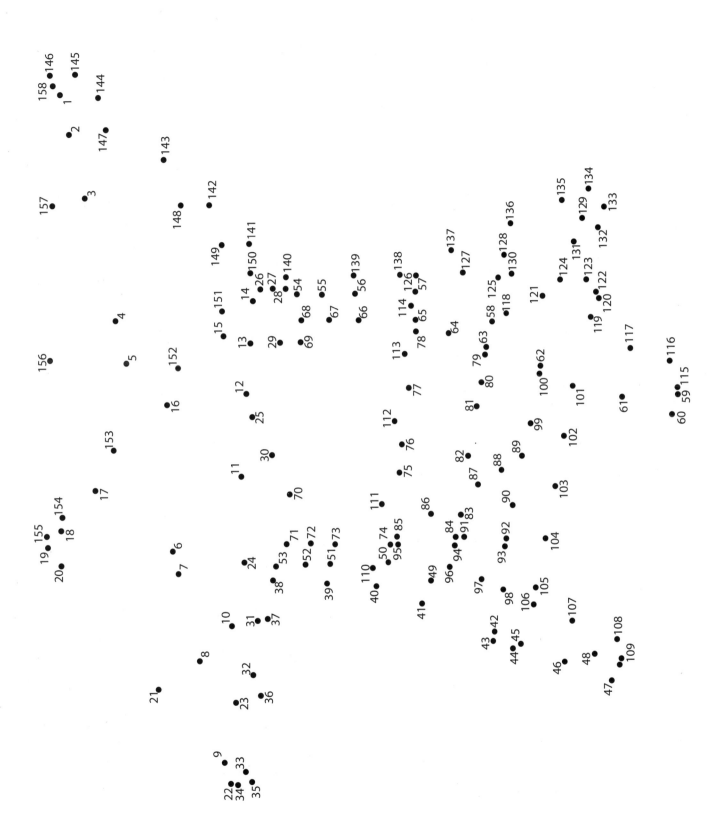

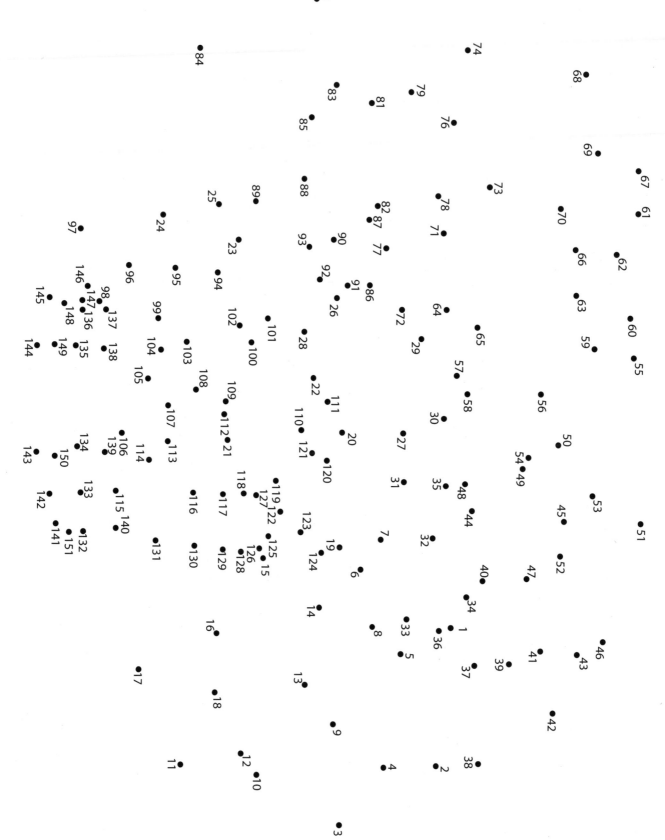

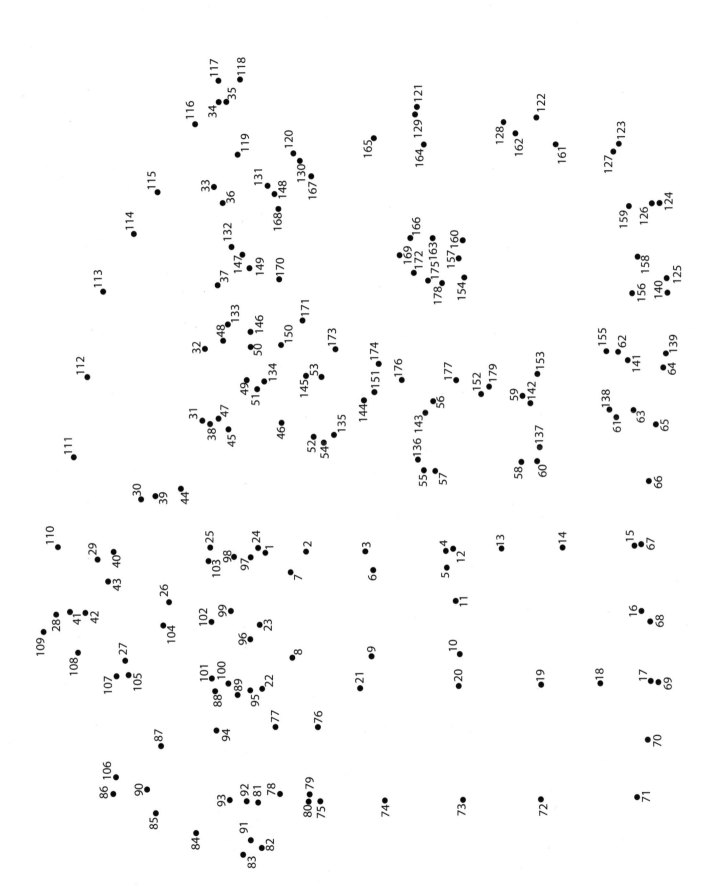

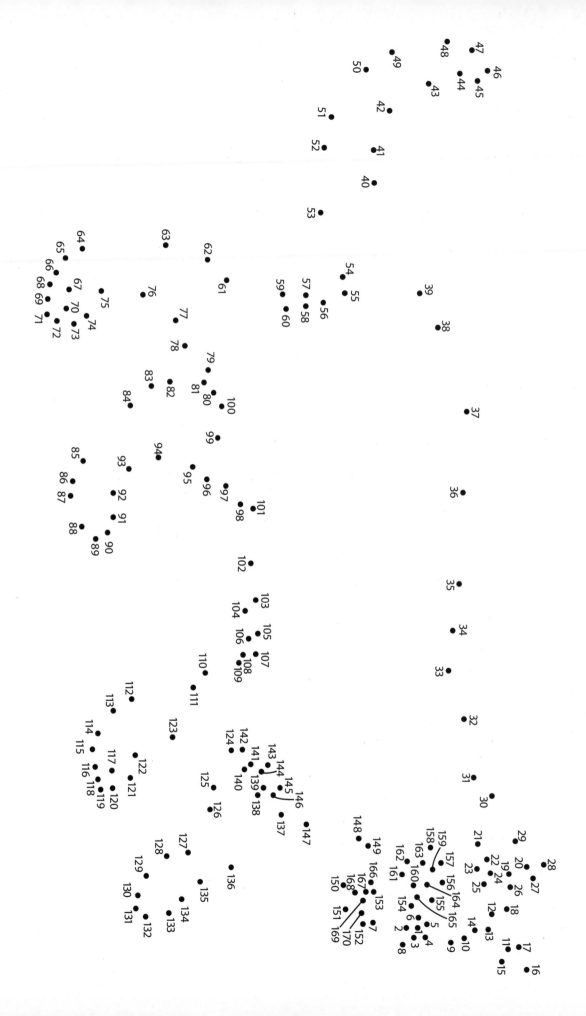

66

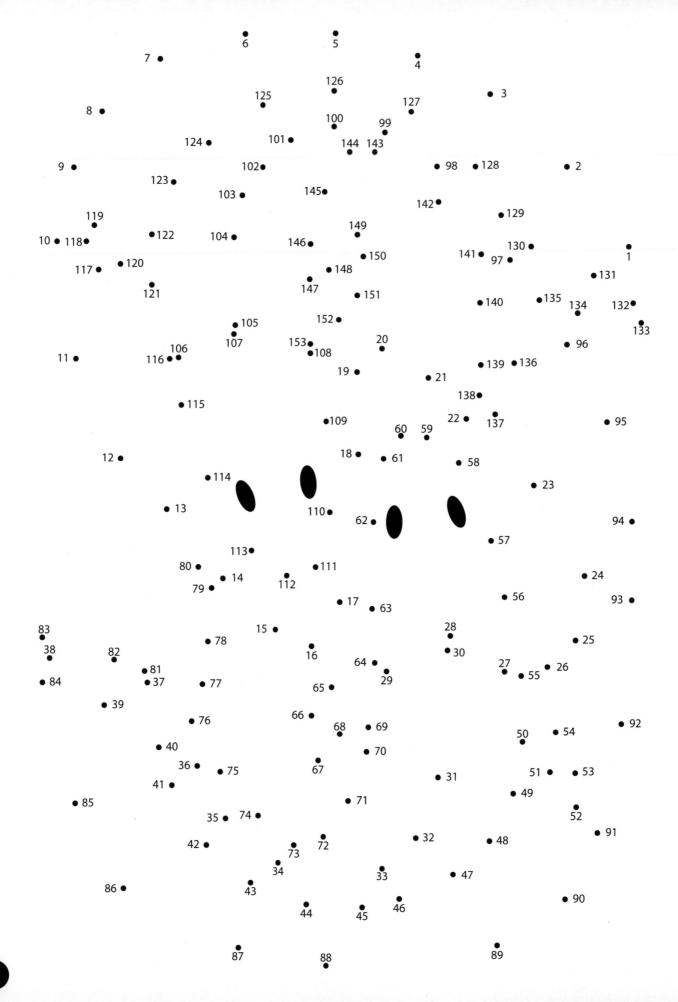

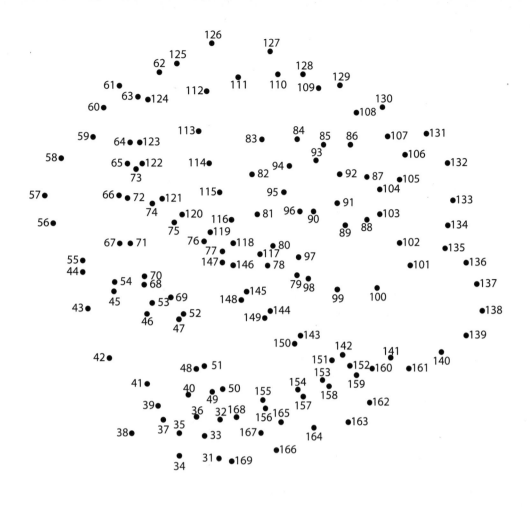
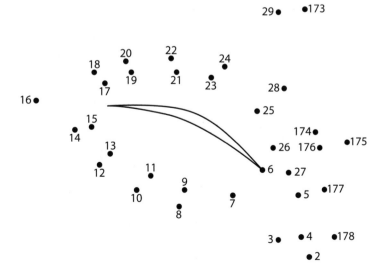

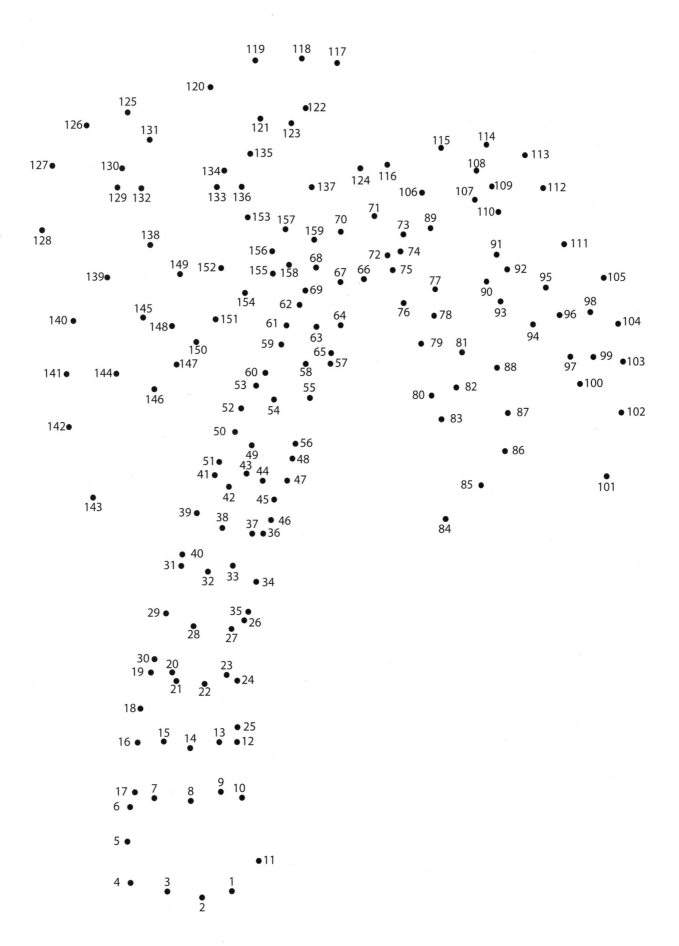

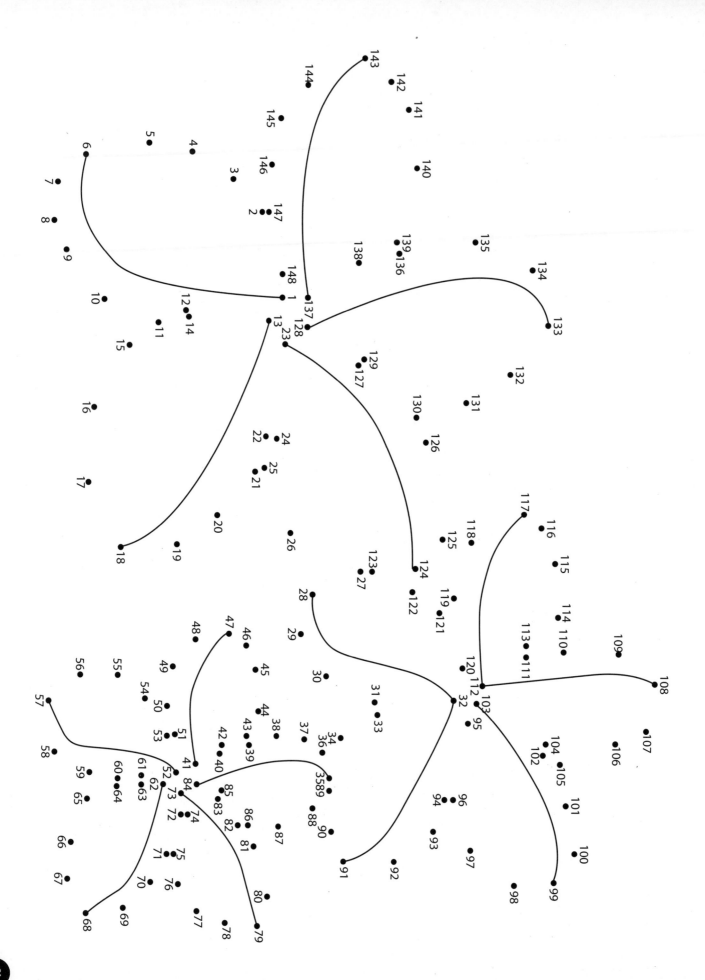

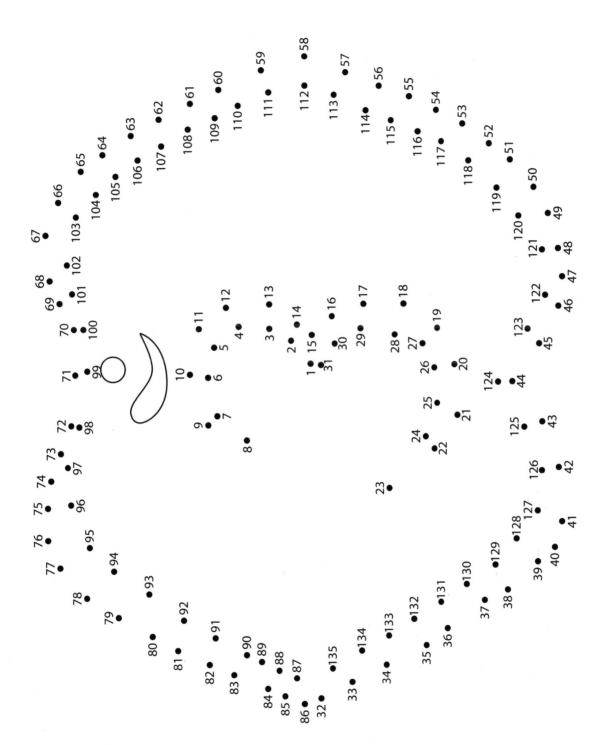

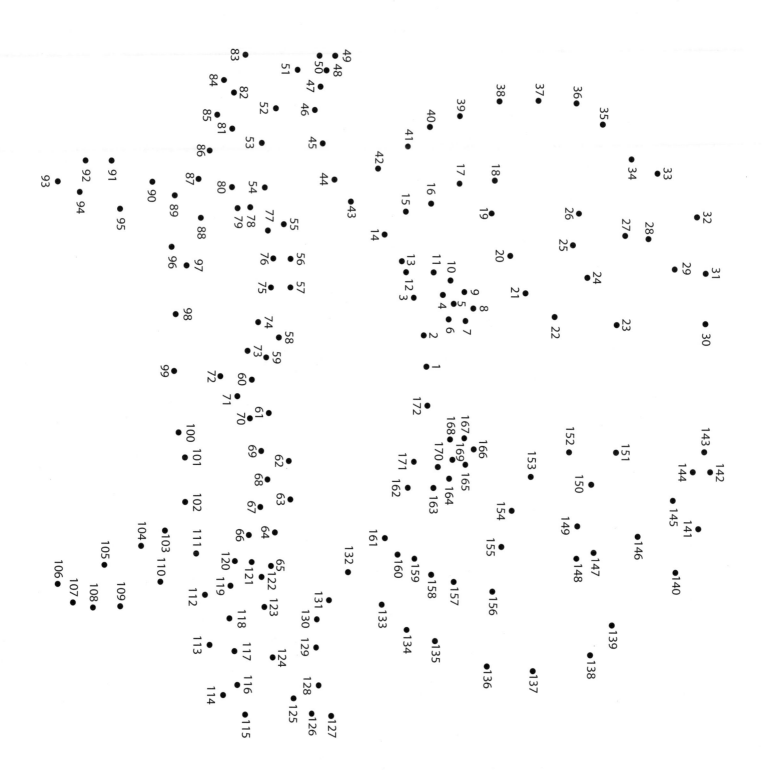

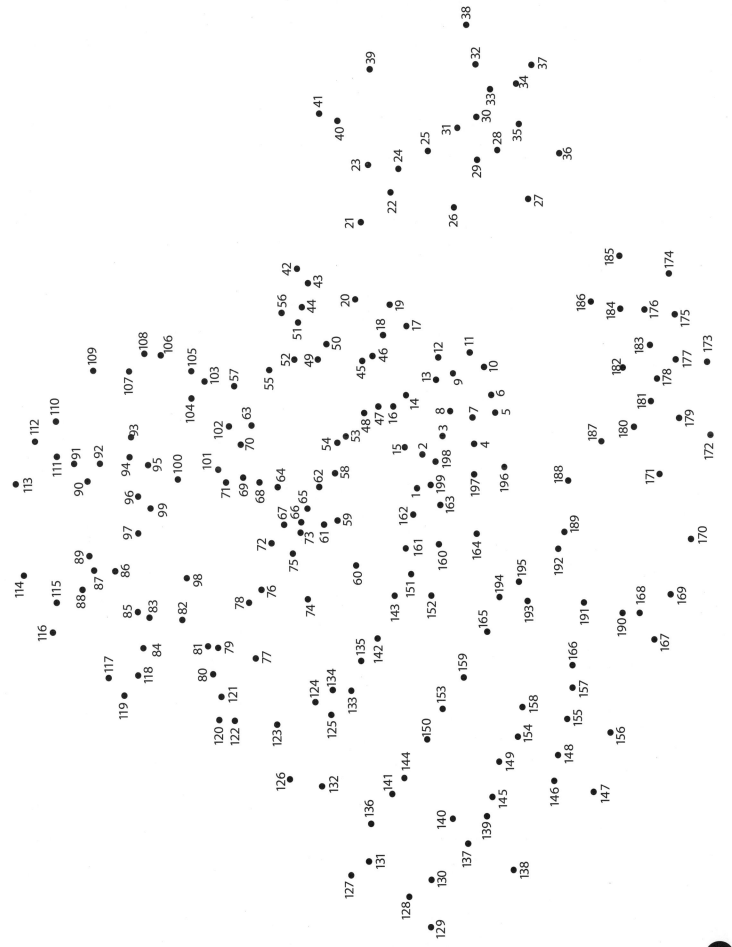

81

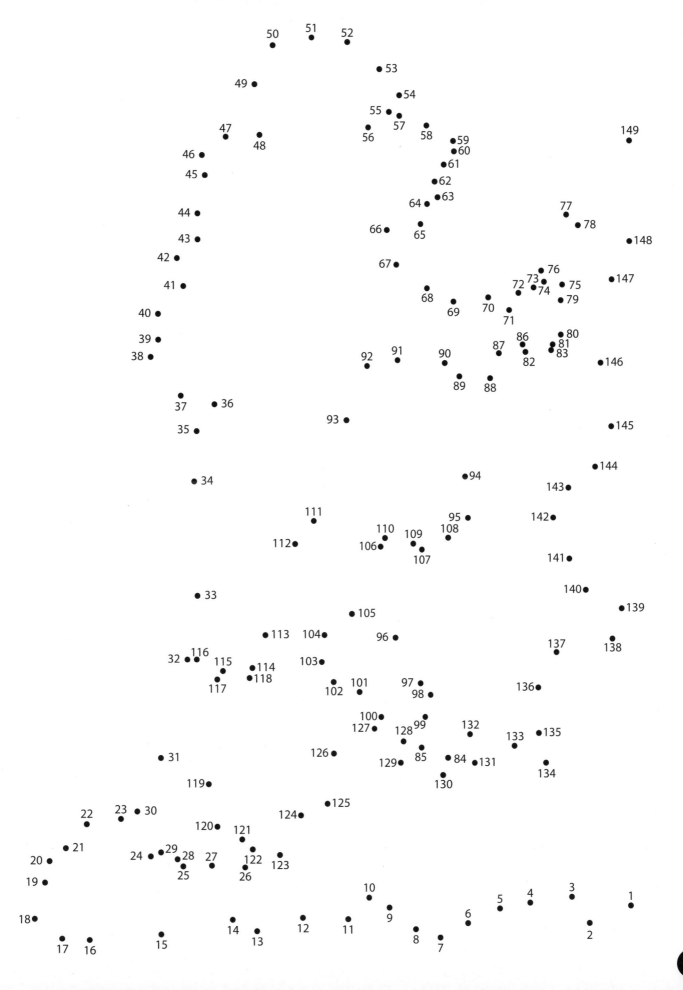

83

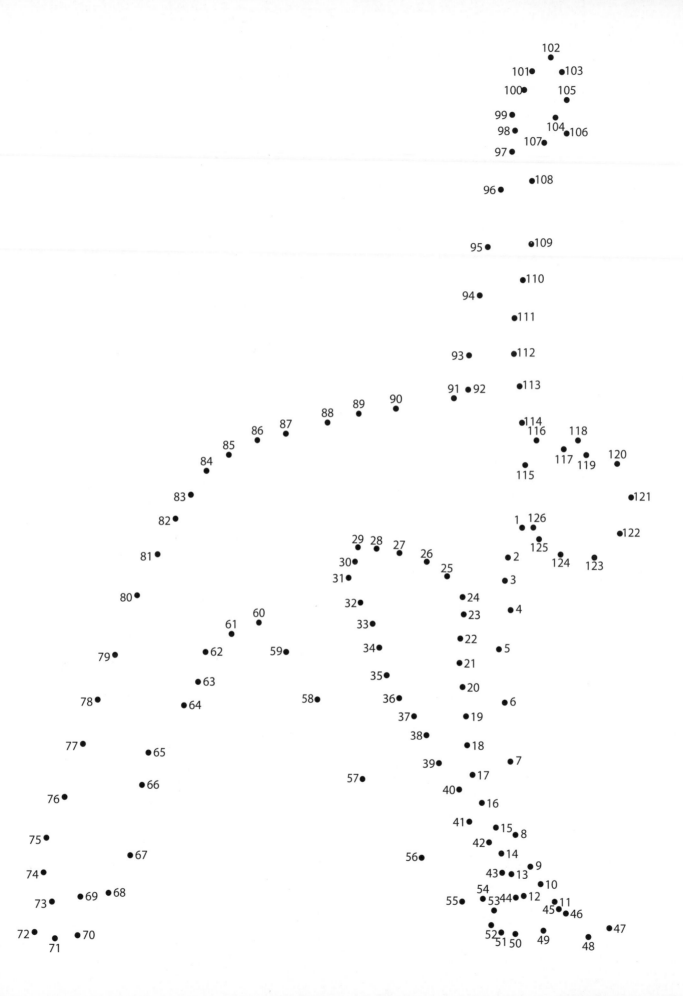

84

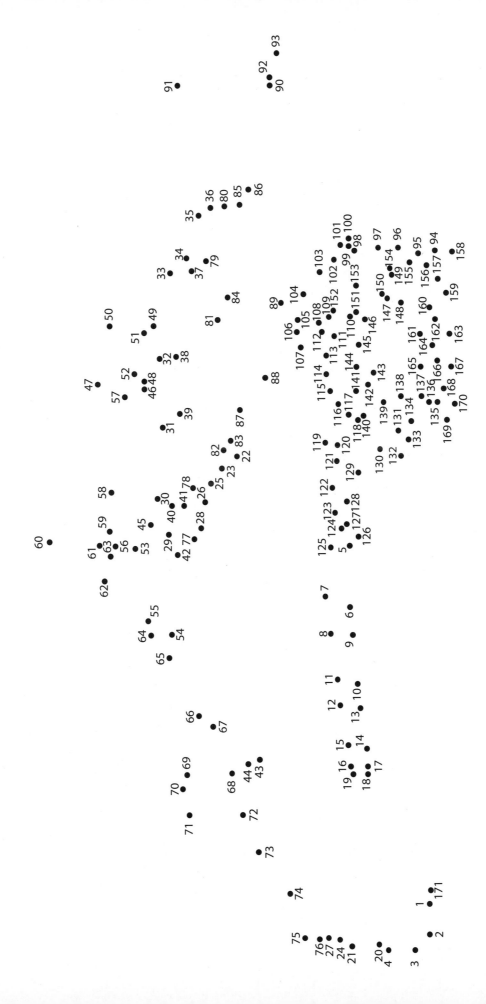

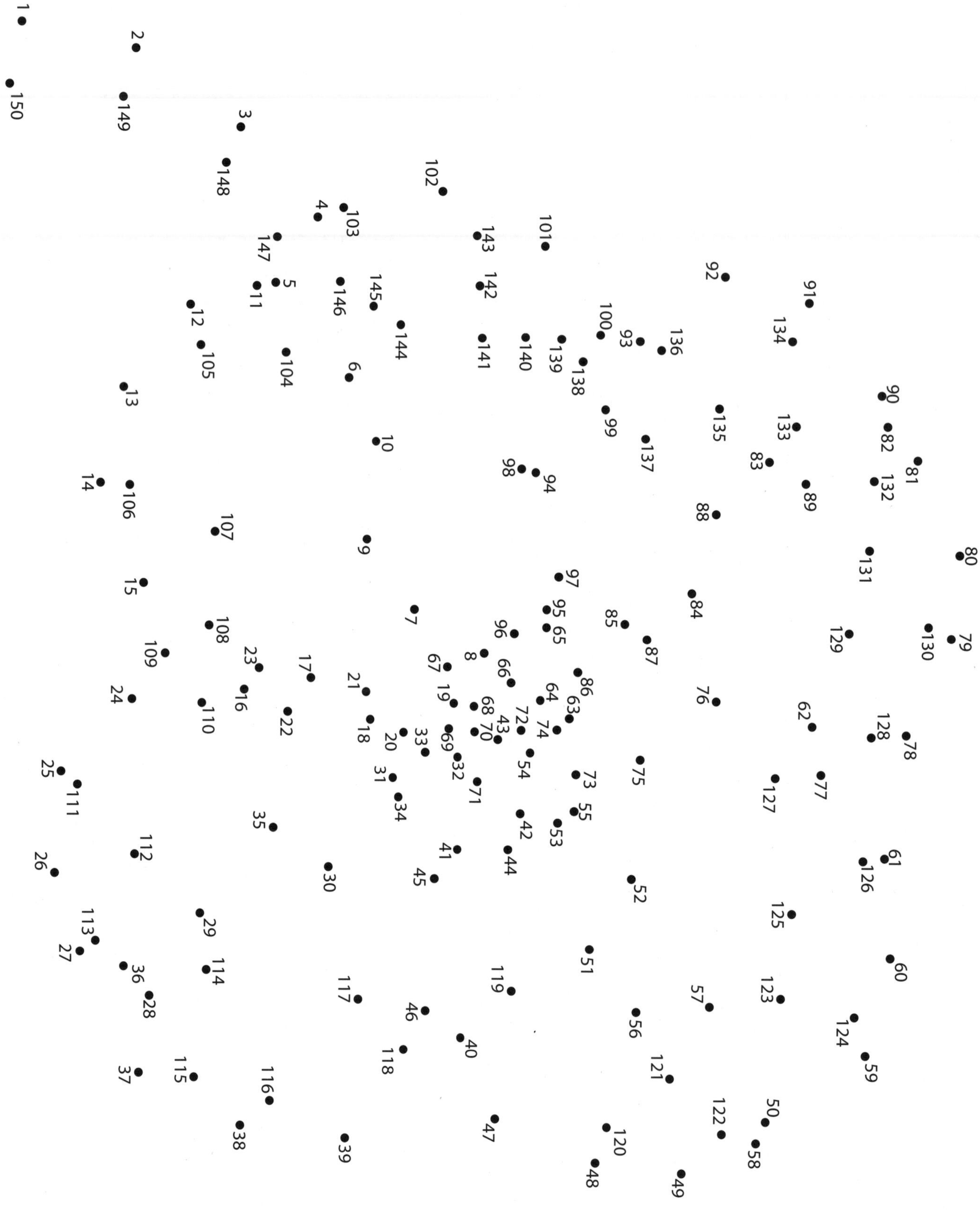

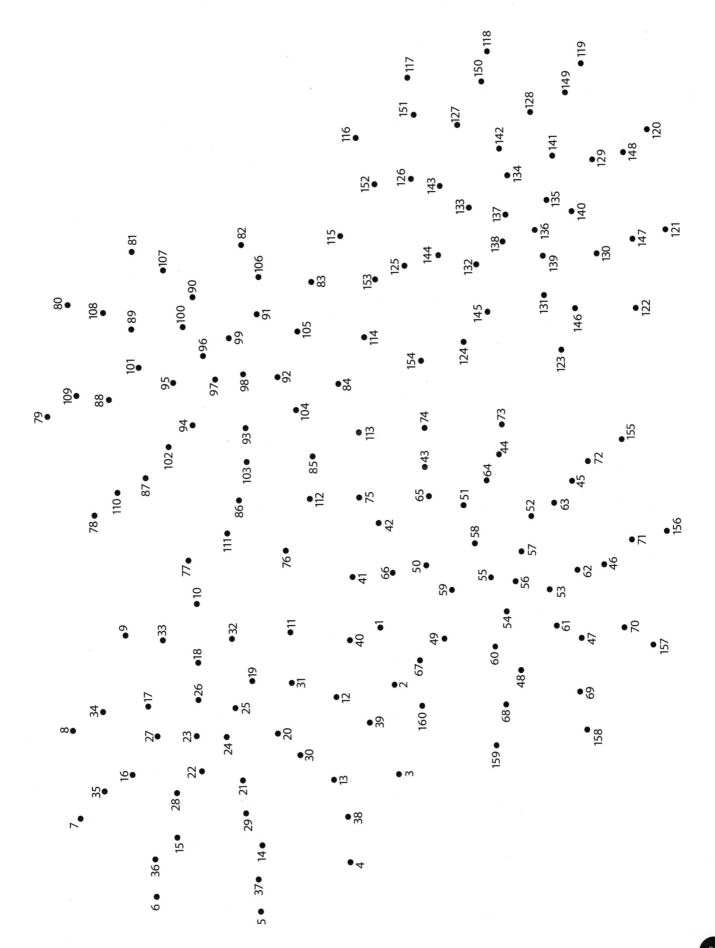

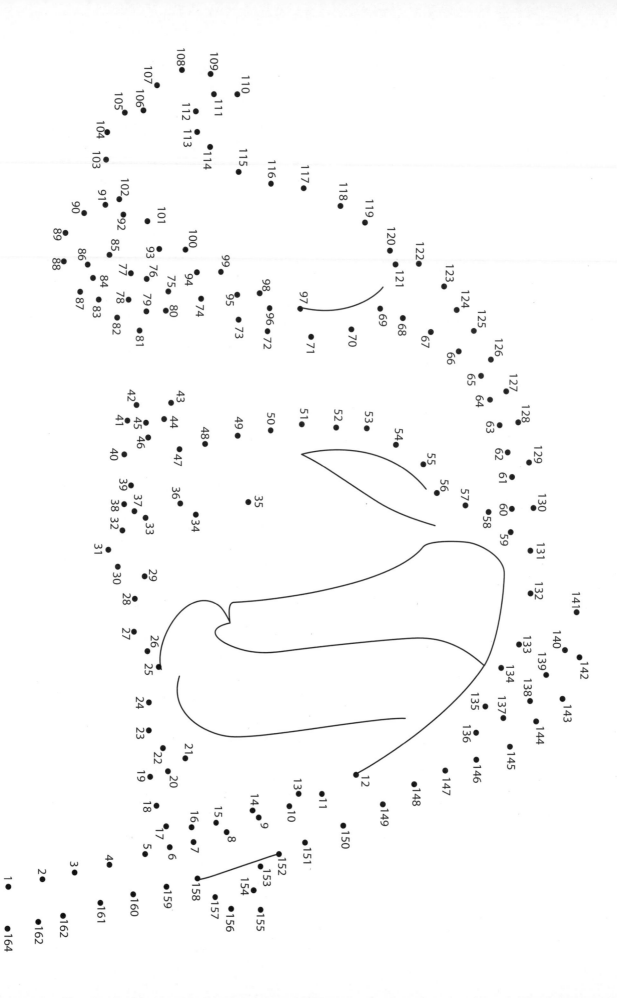

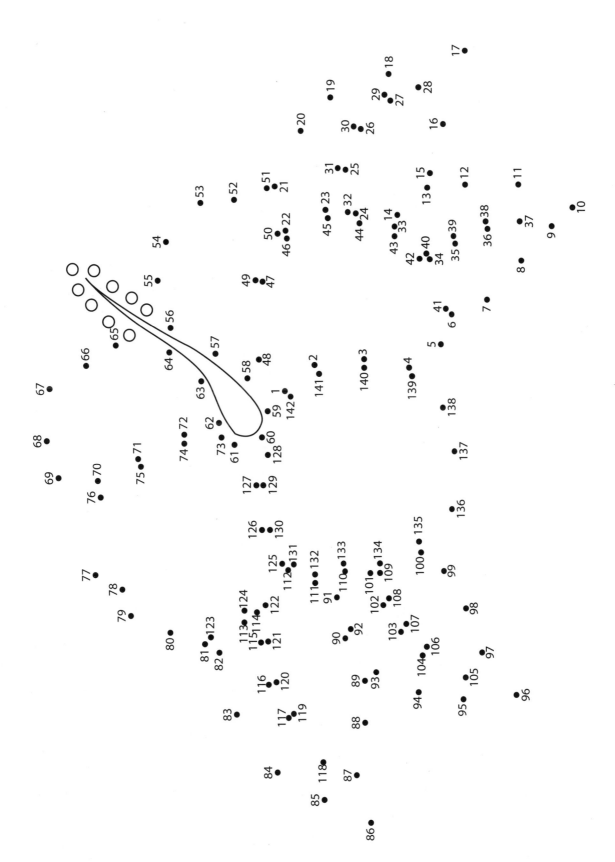

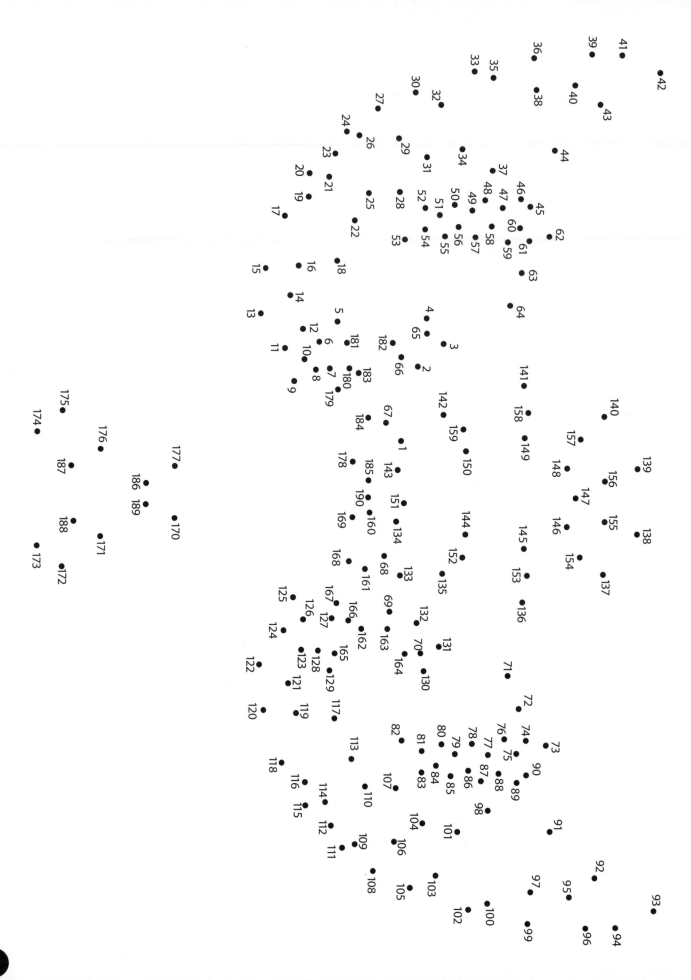

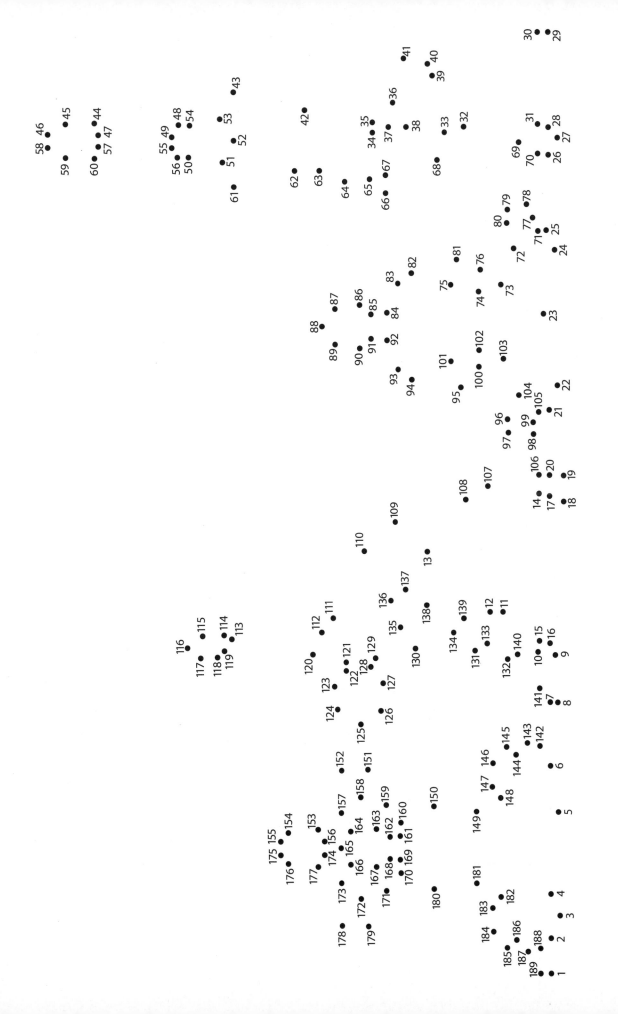

93

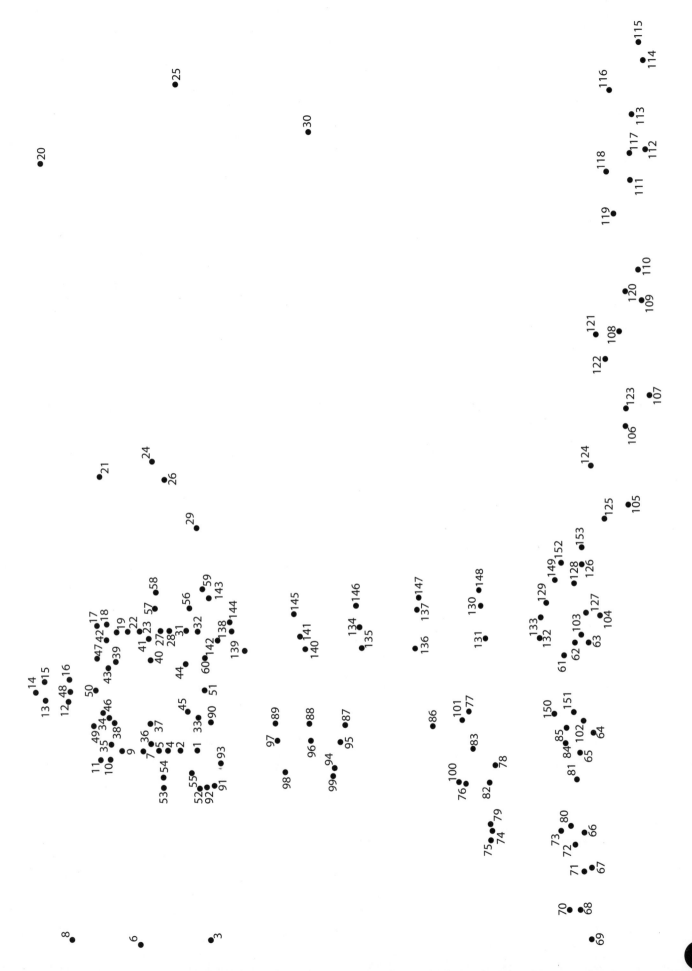

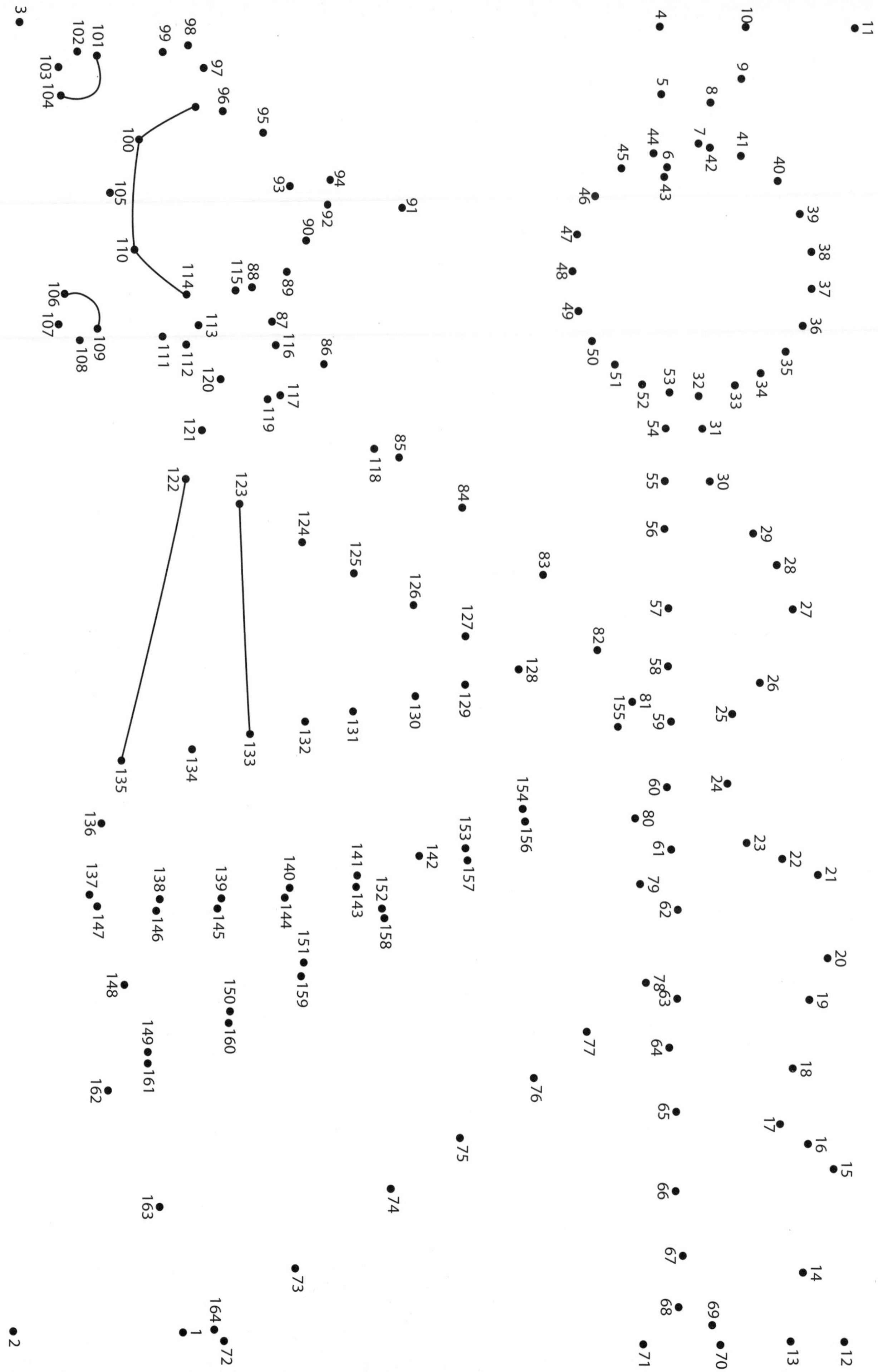

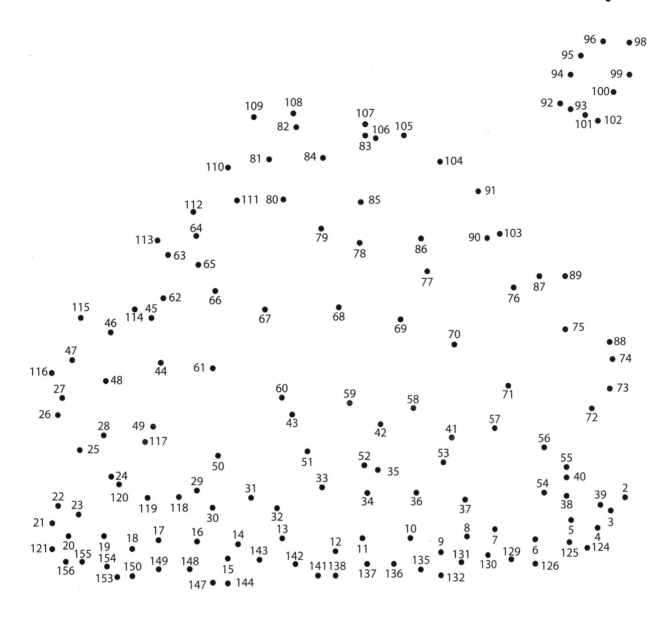

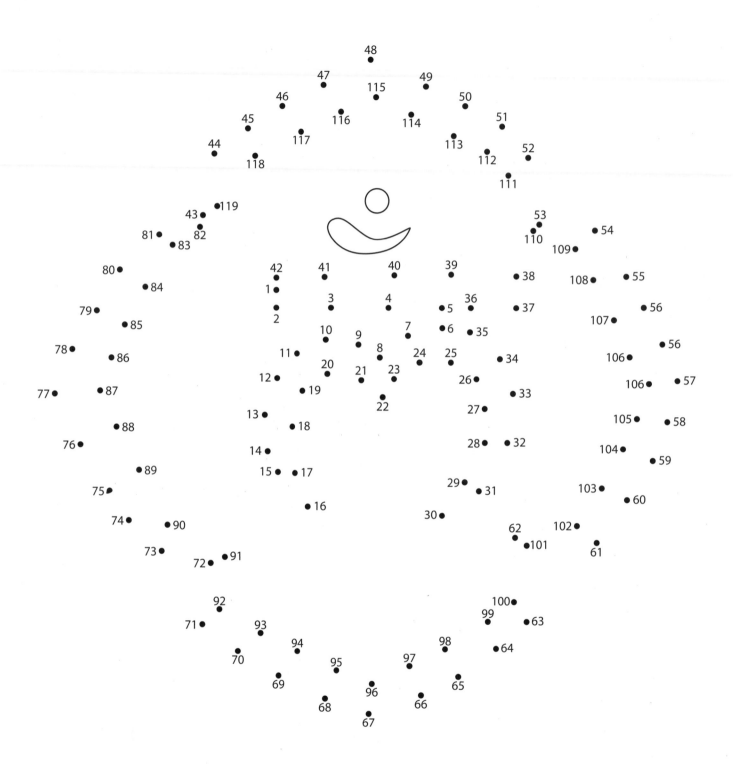

99

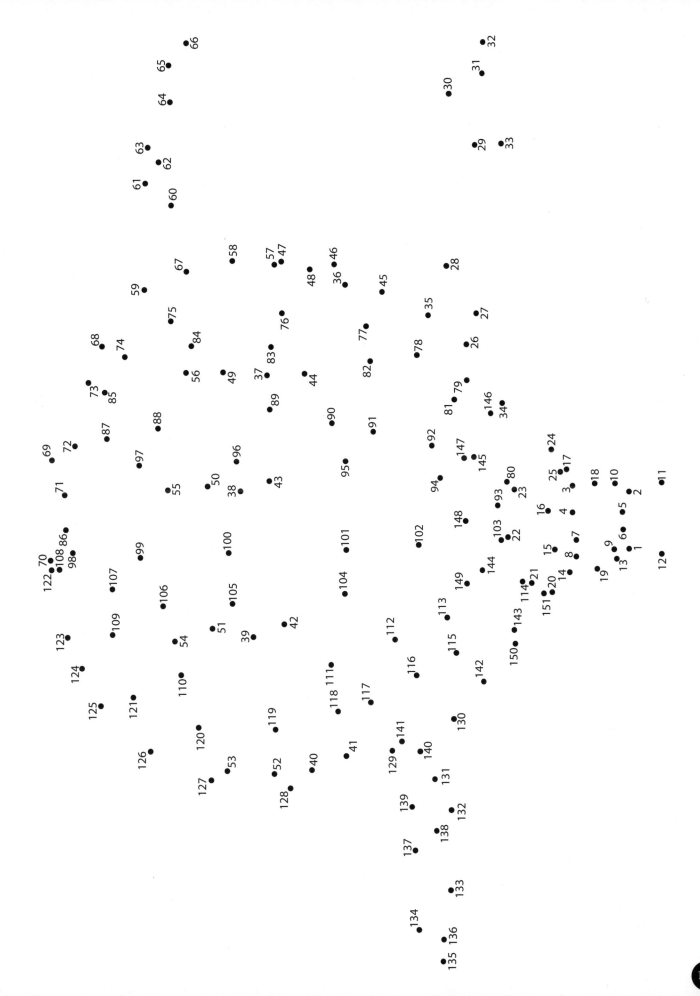

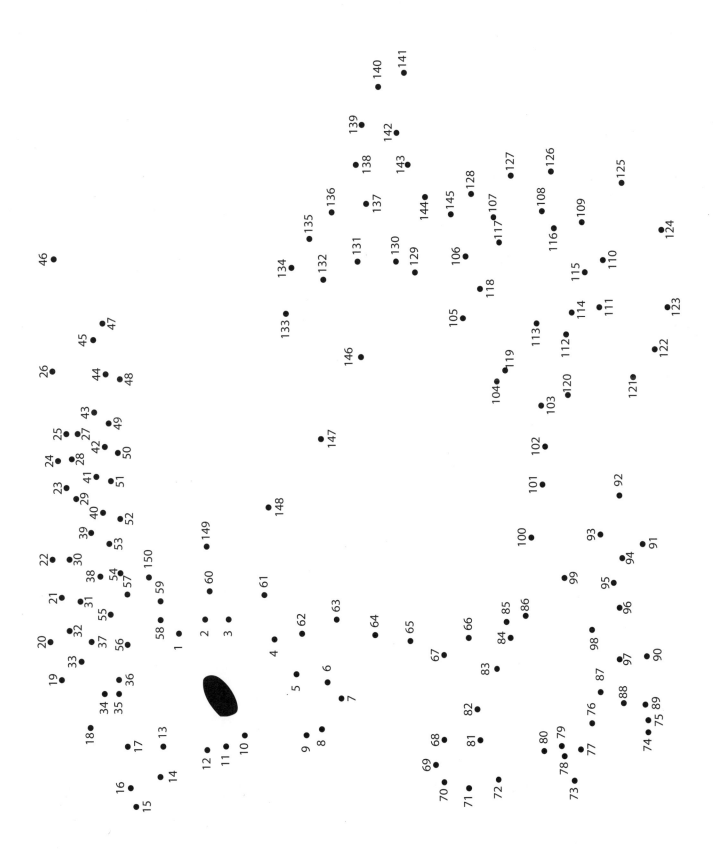

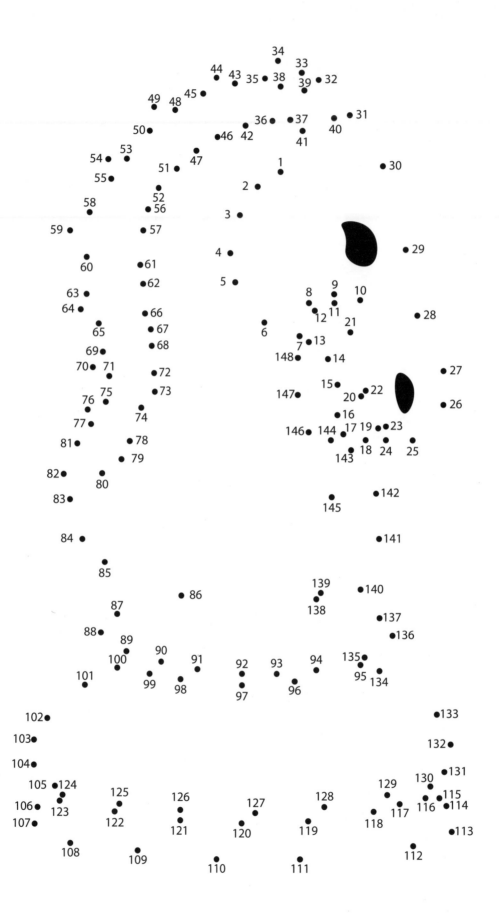

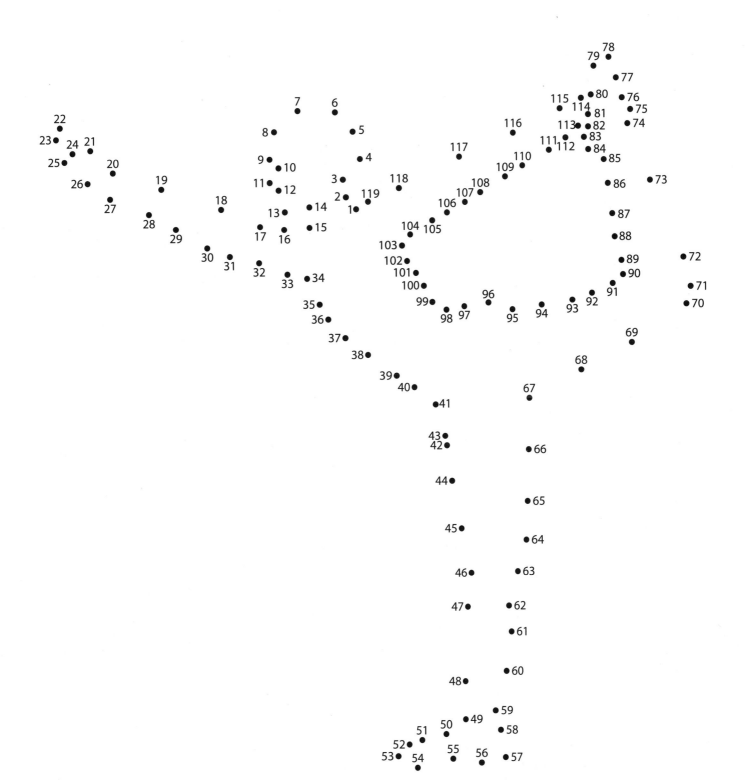

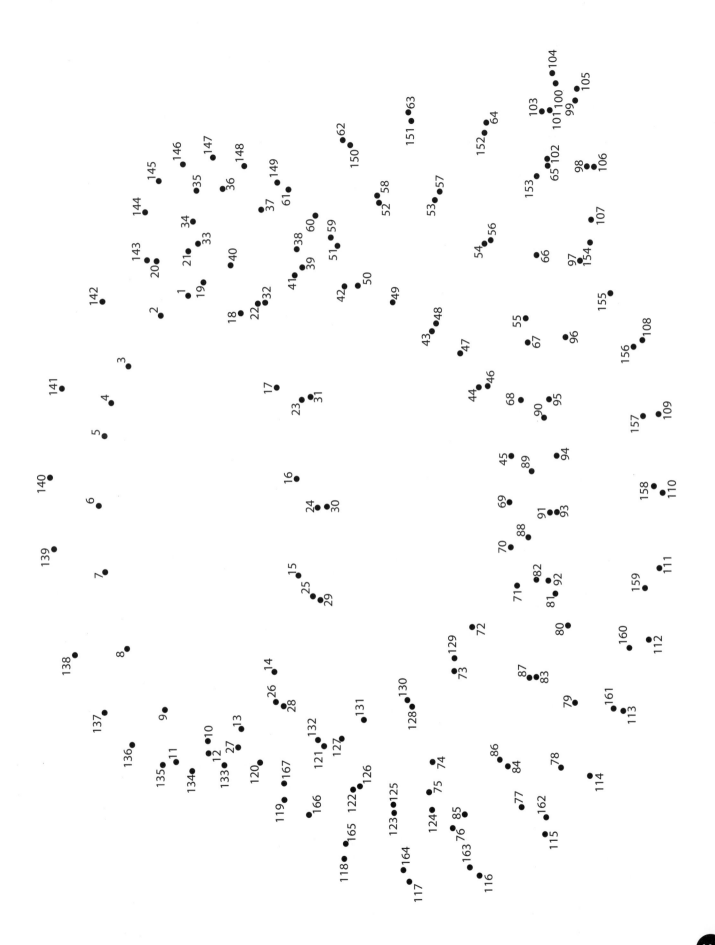

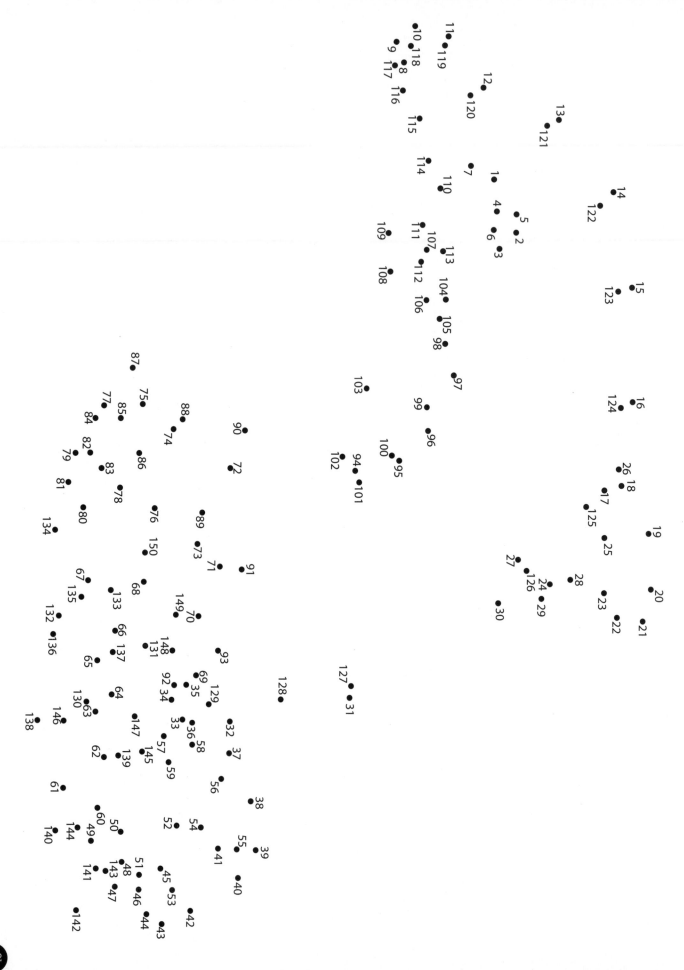

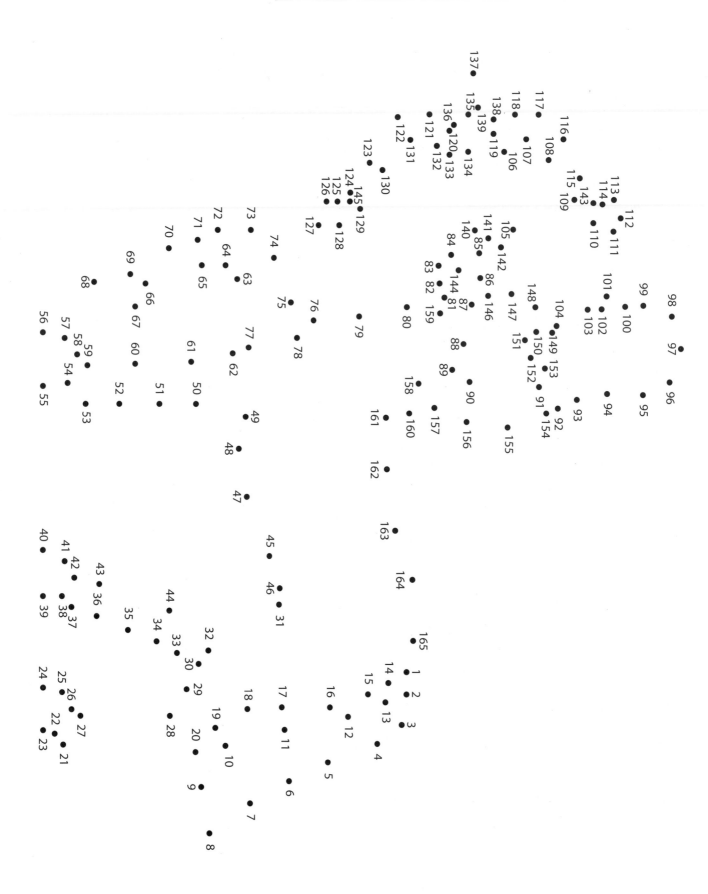

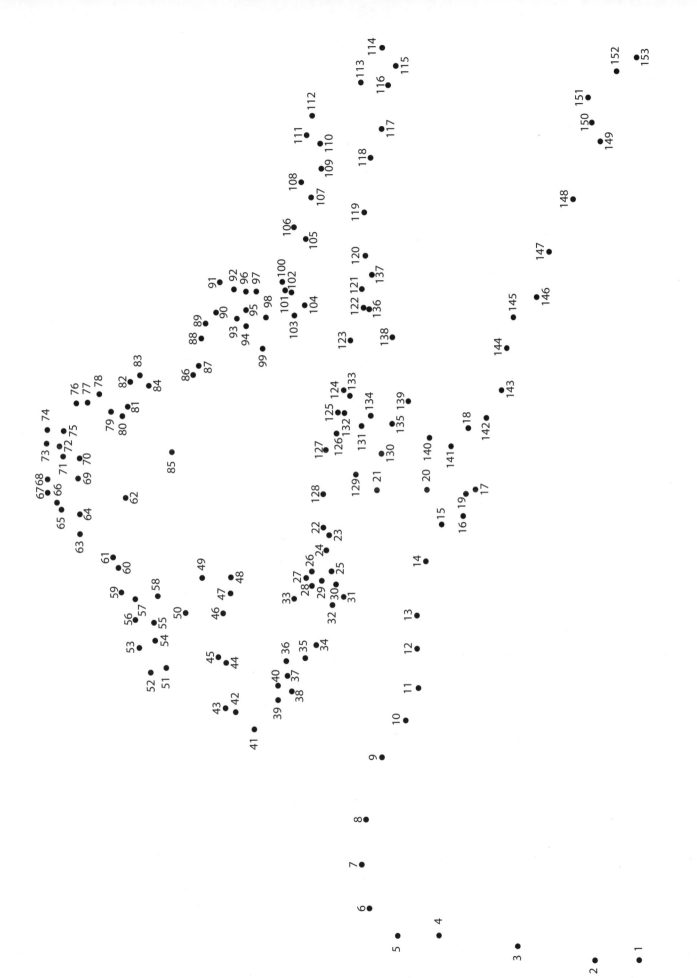

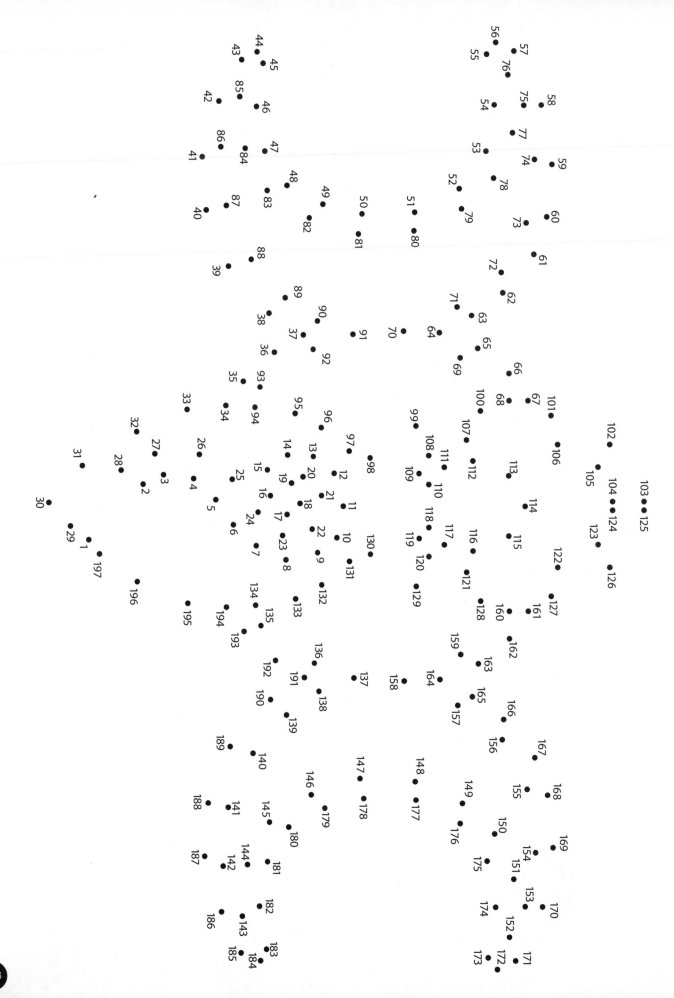

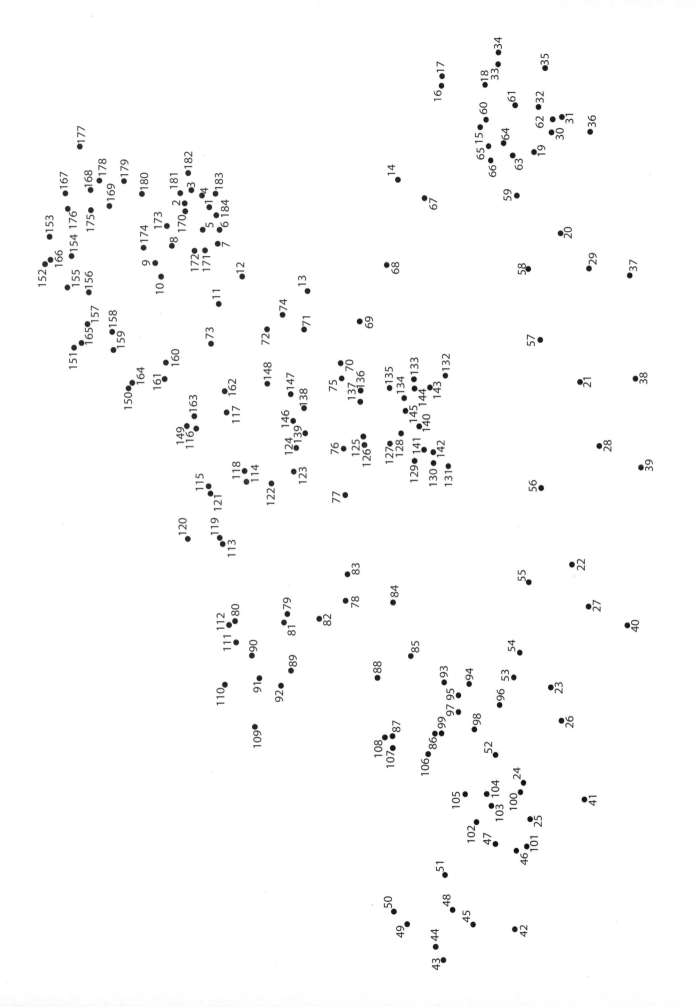

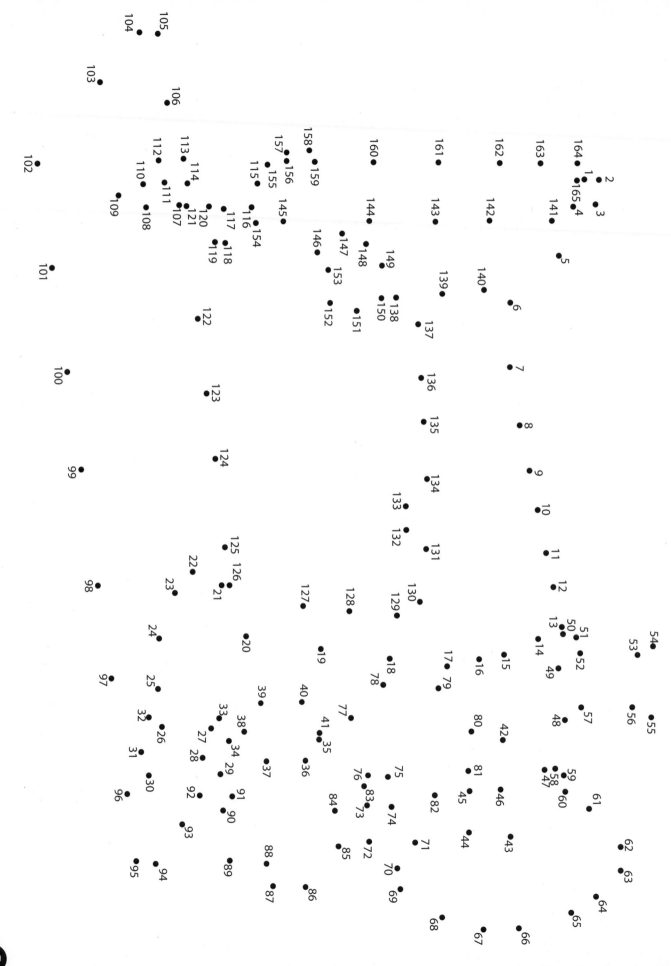

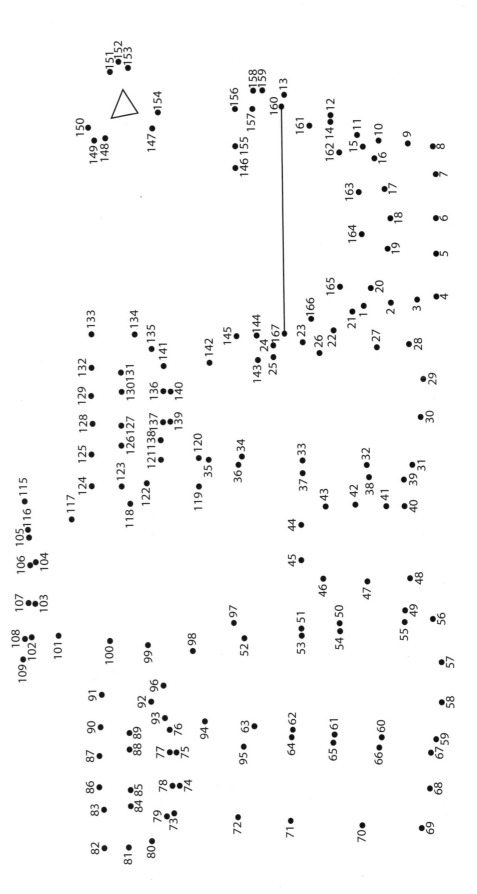

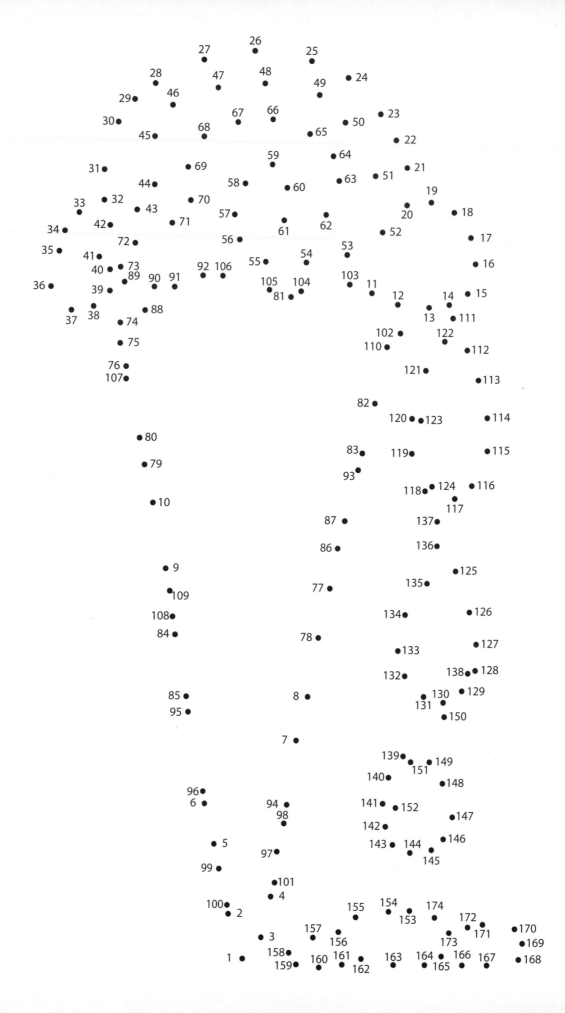

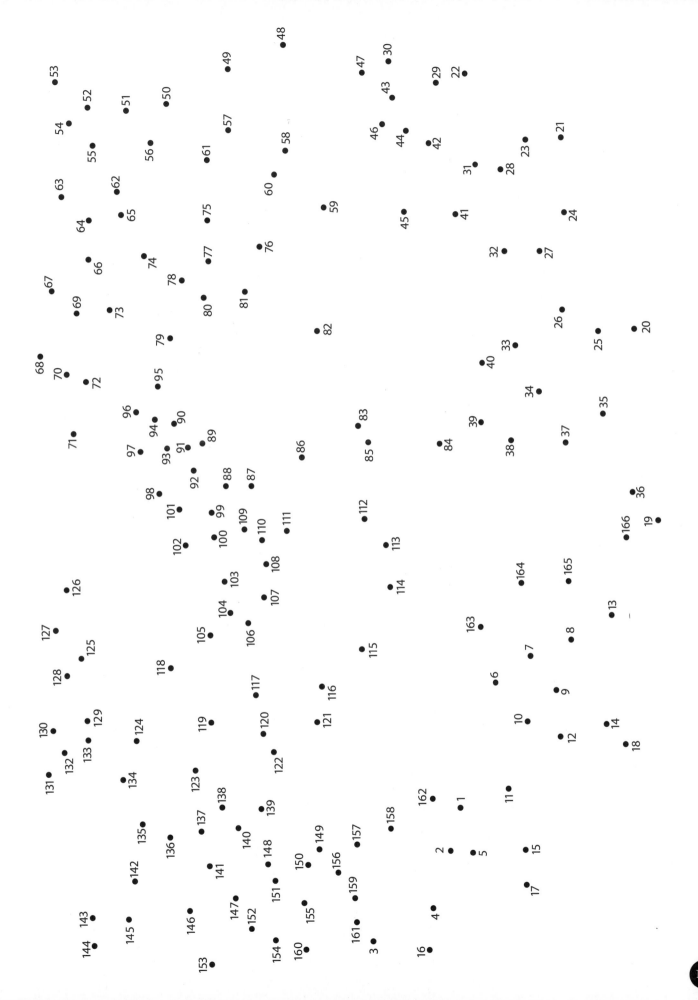

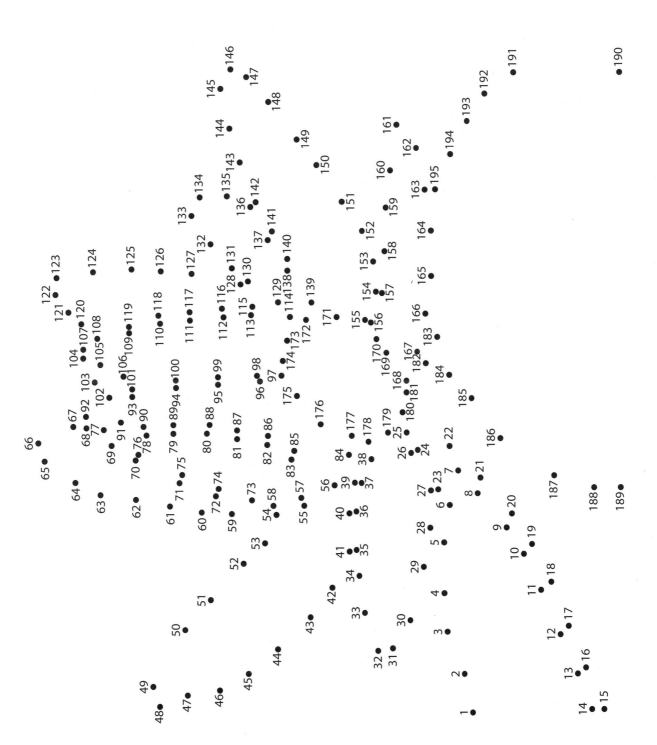

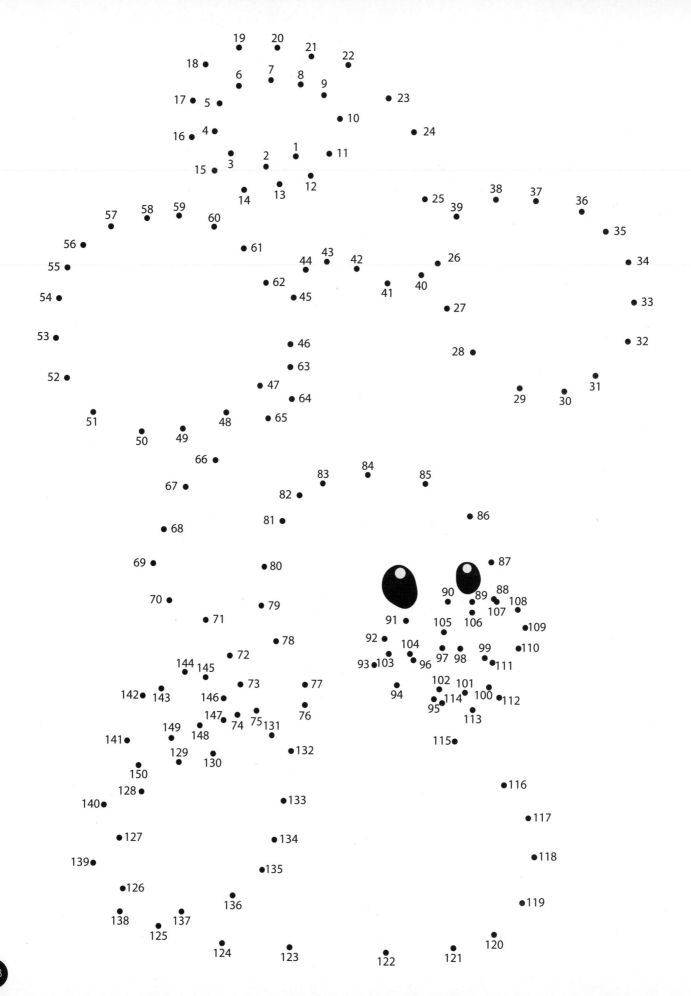

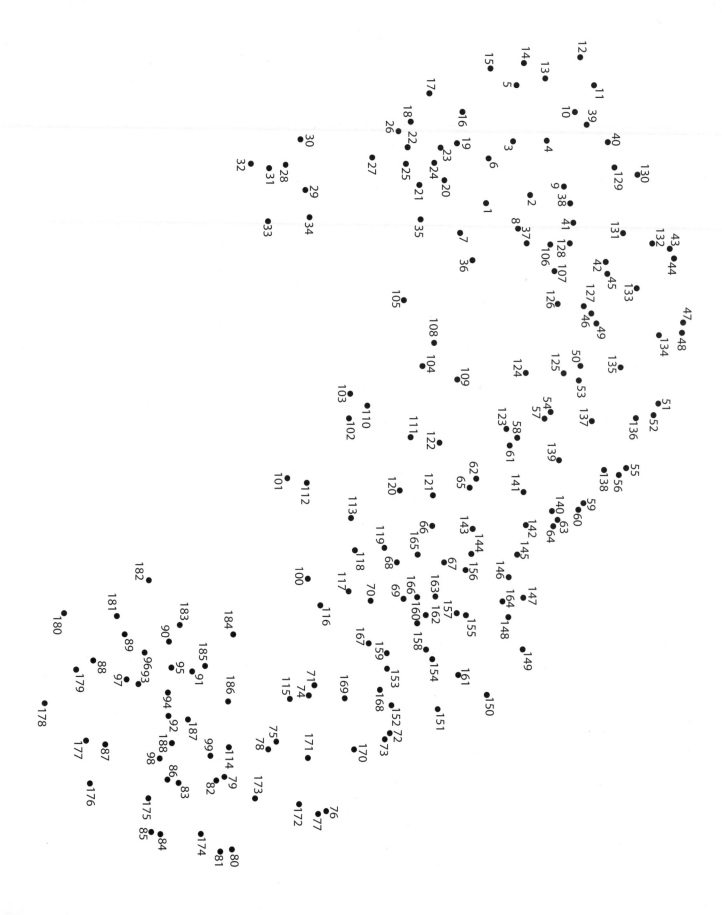

130

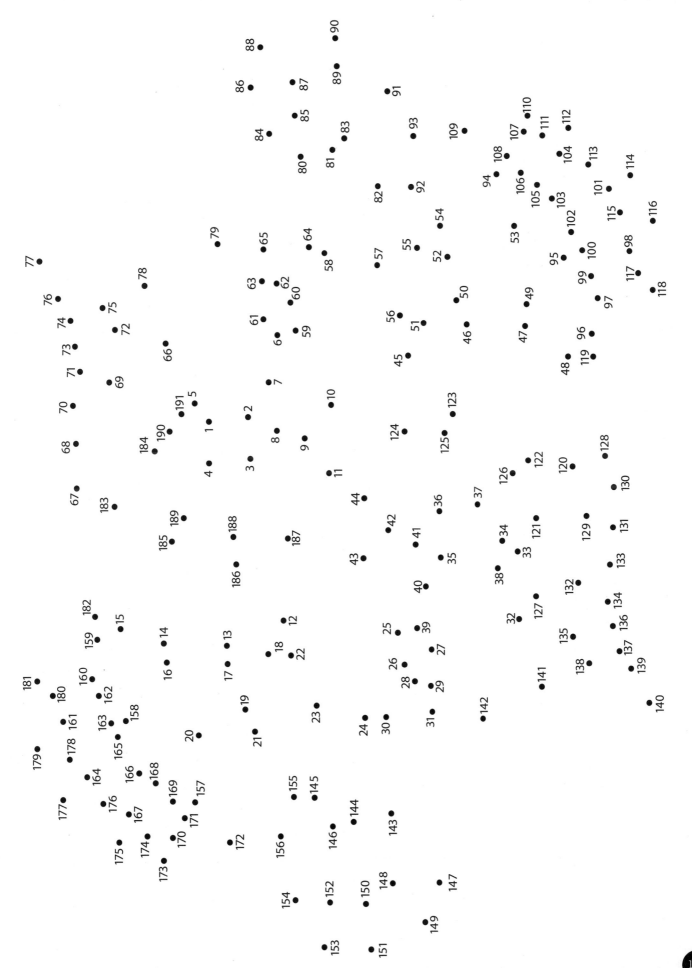

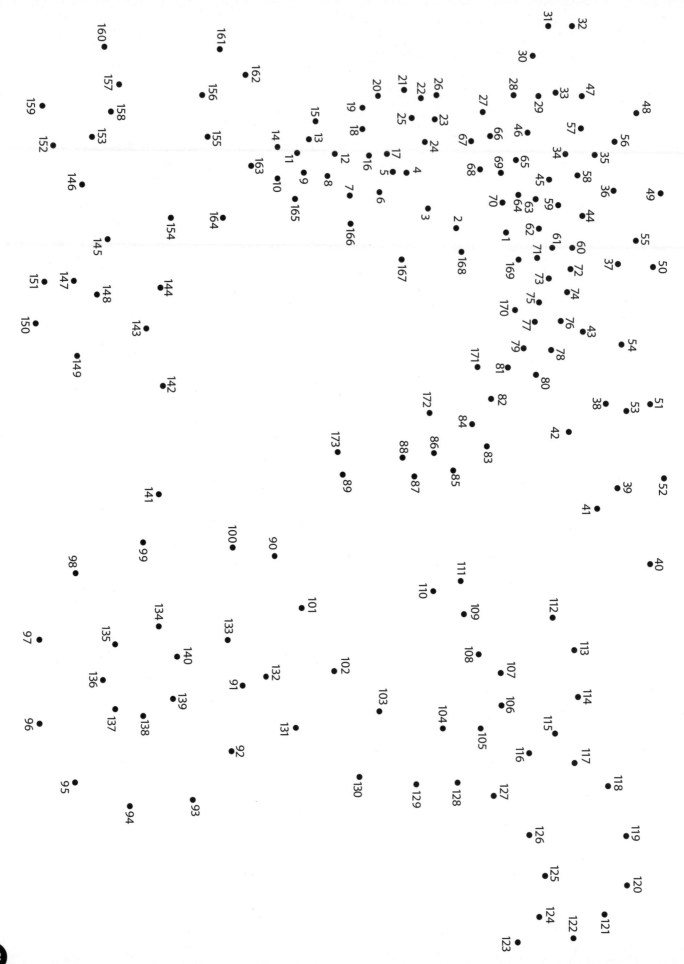

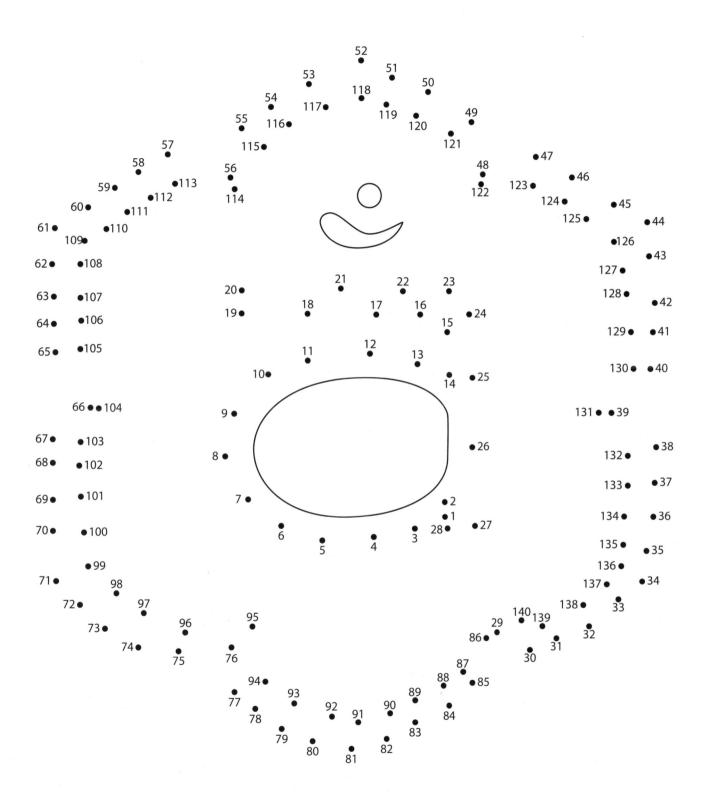

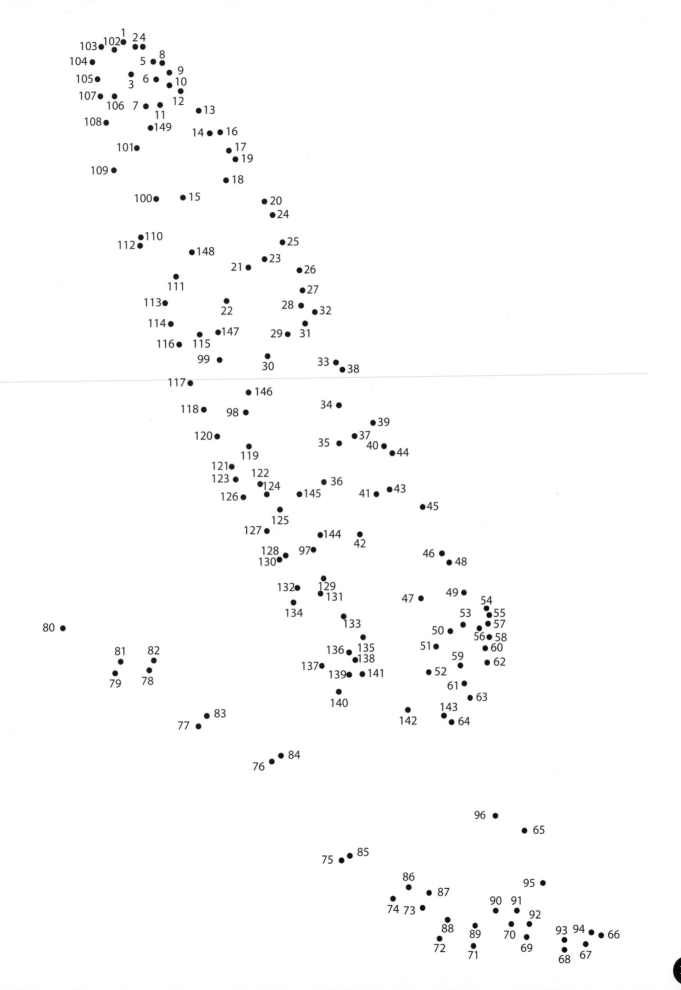

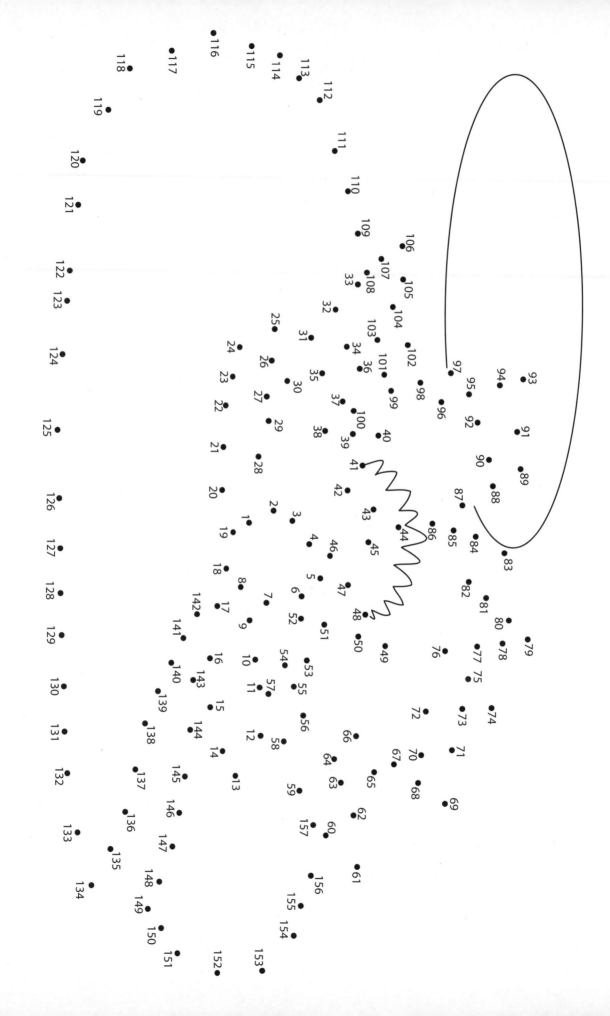

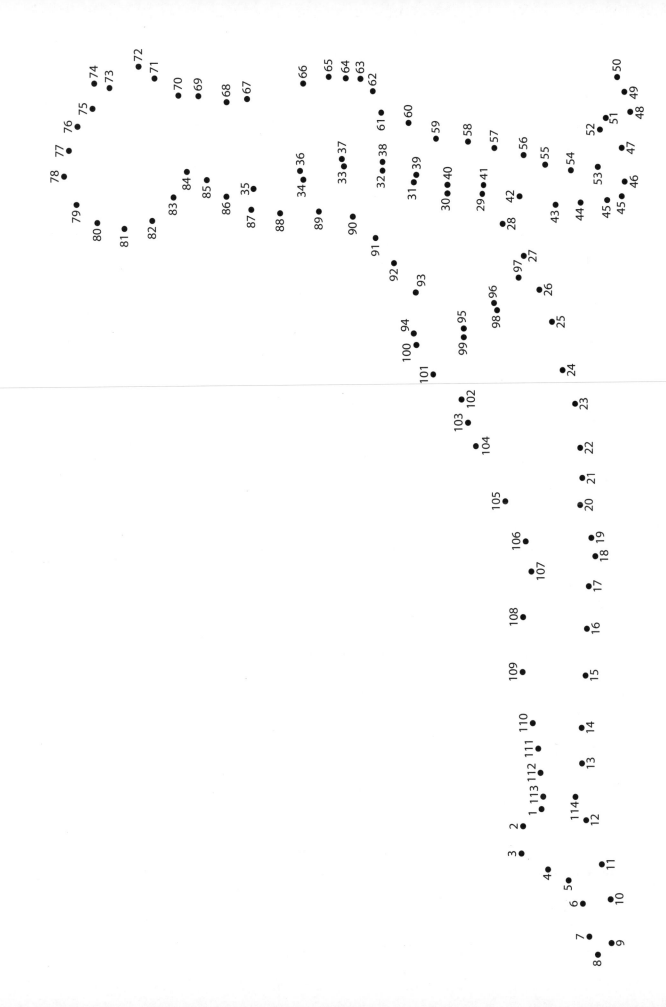

138

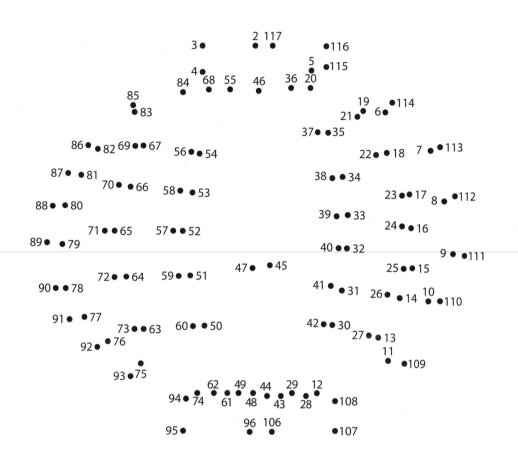
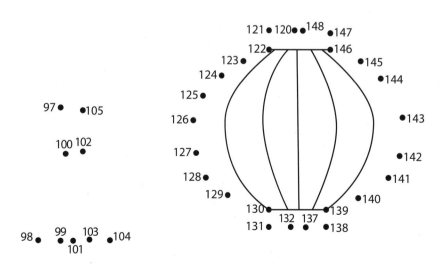

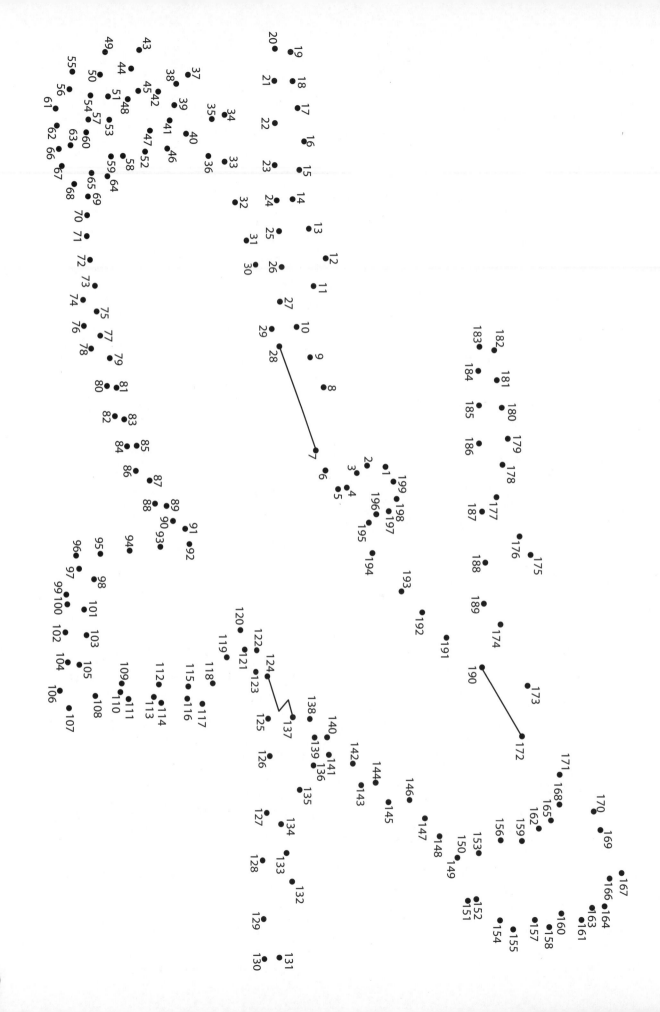

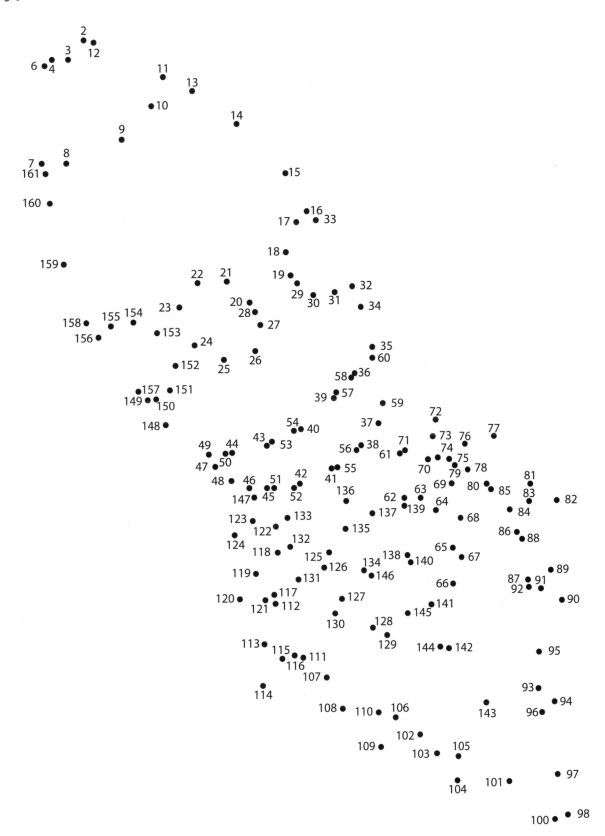

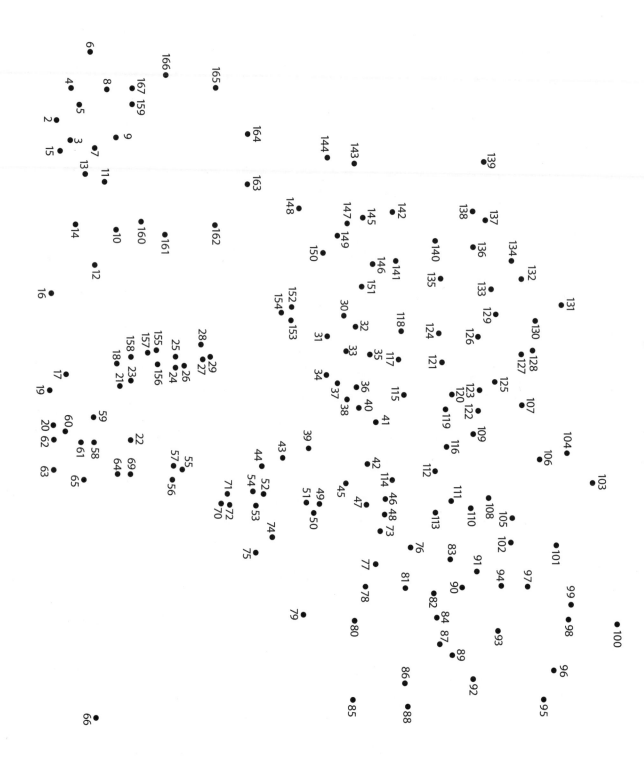

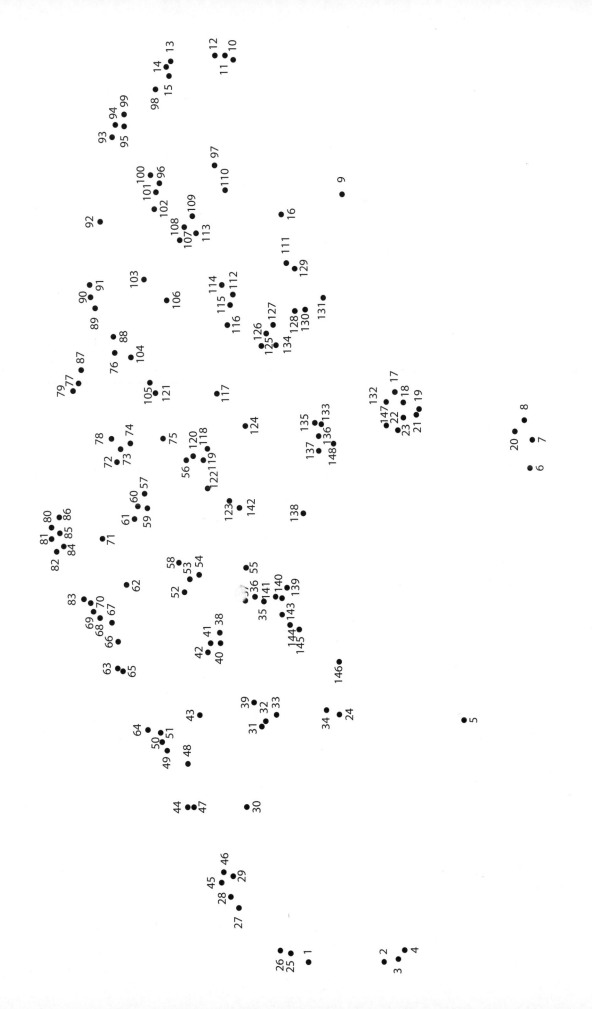

143

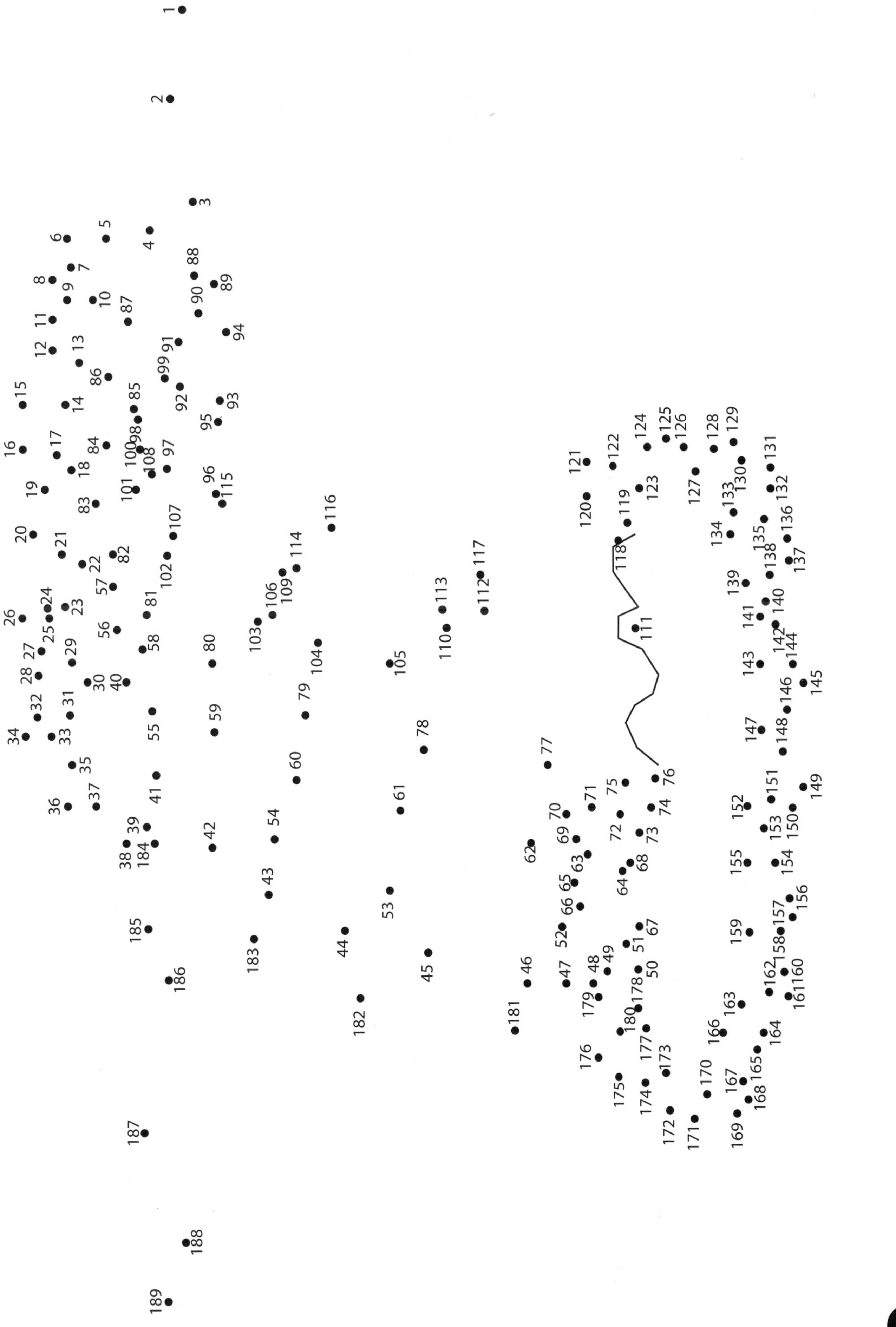

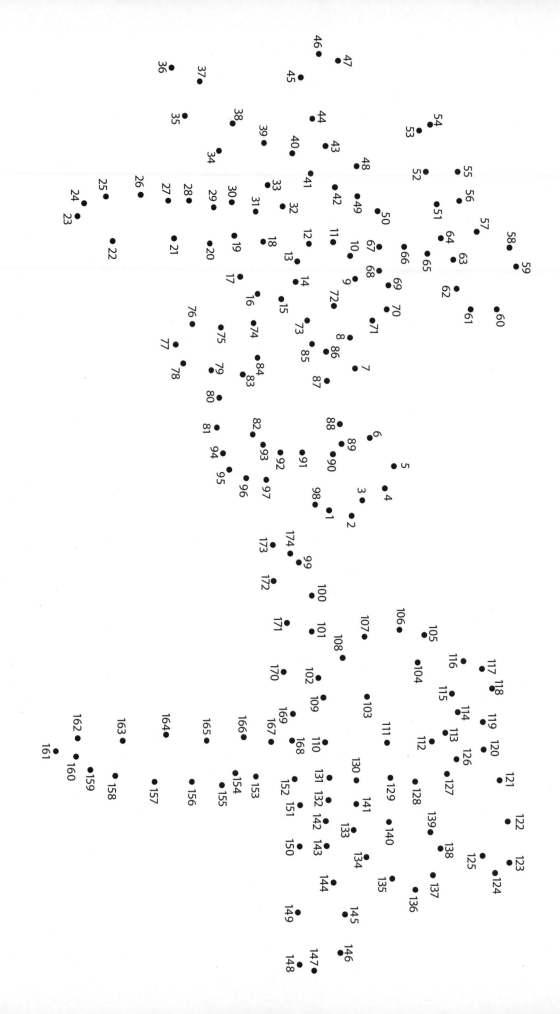

147

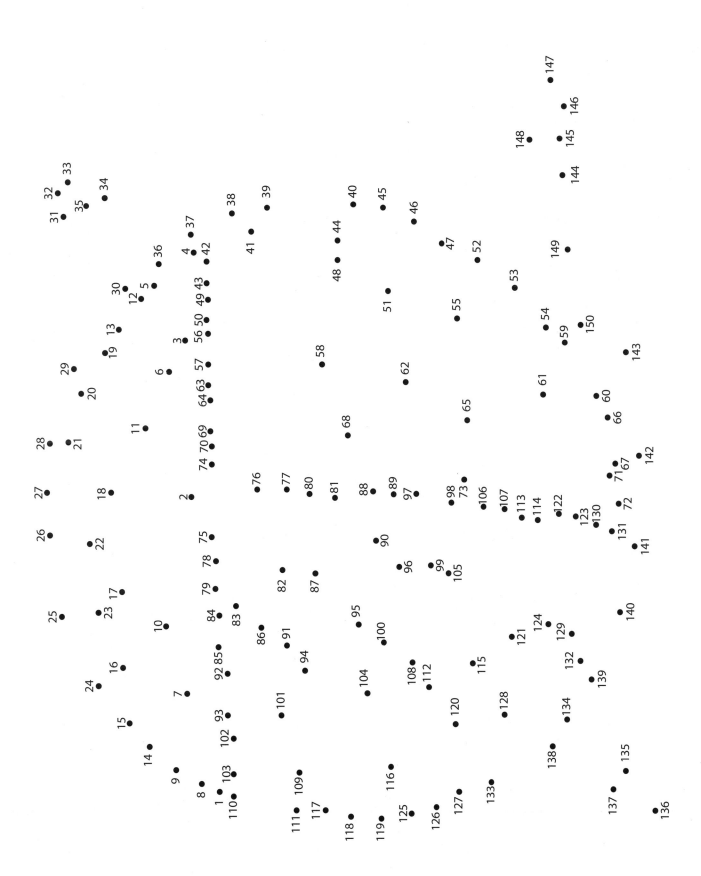

149

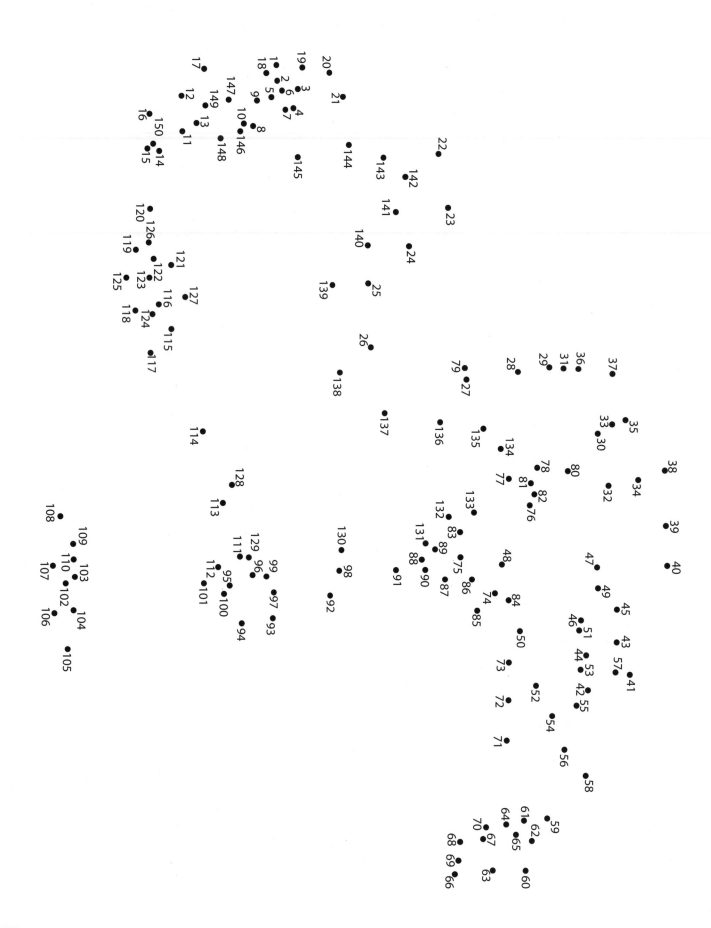

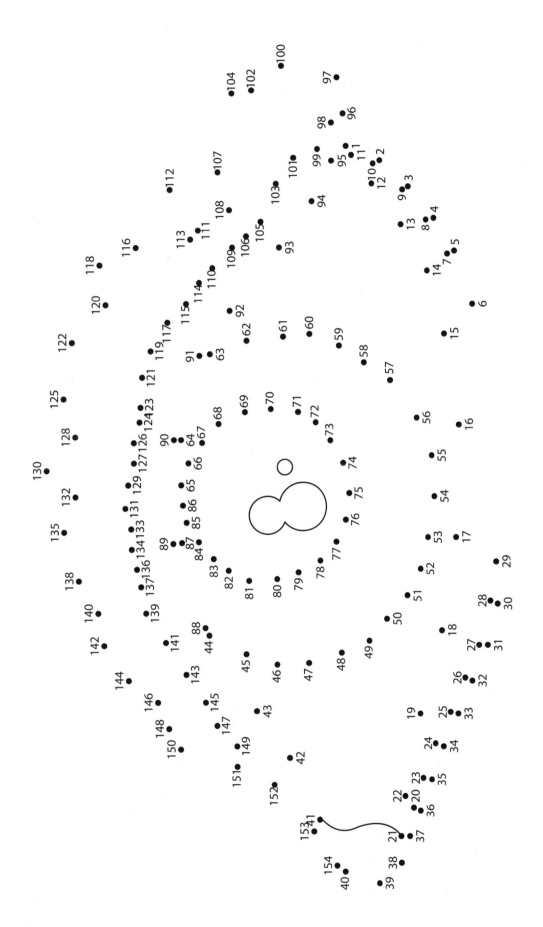

152

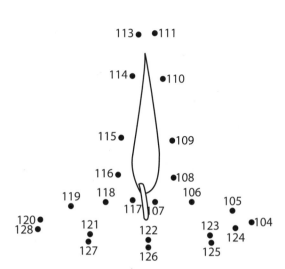
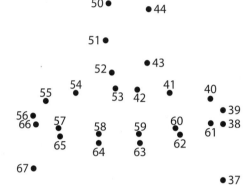
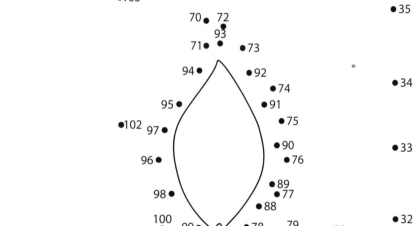
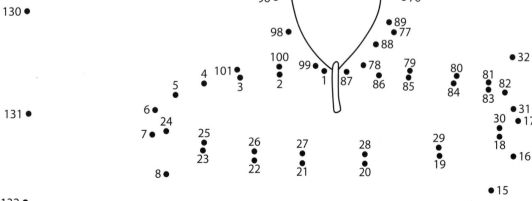

153

154

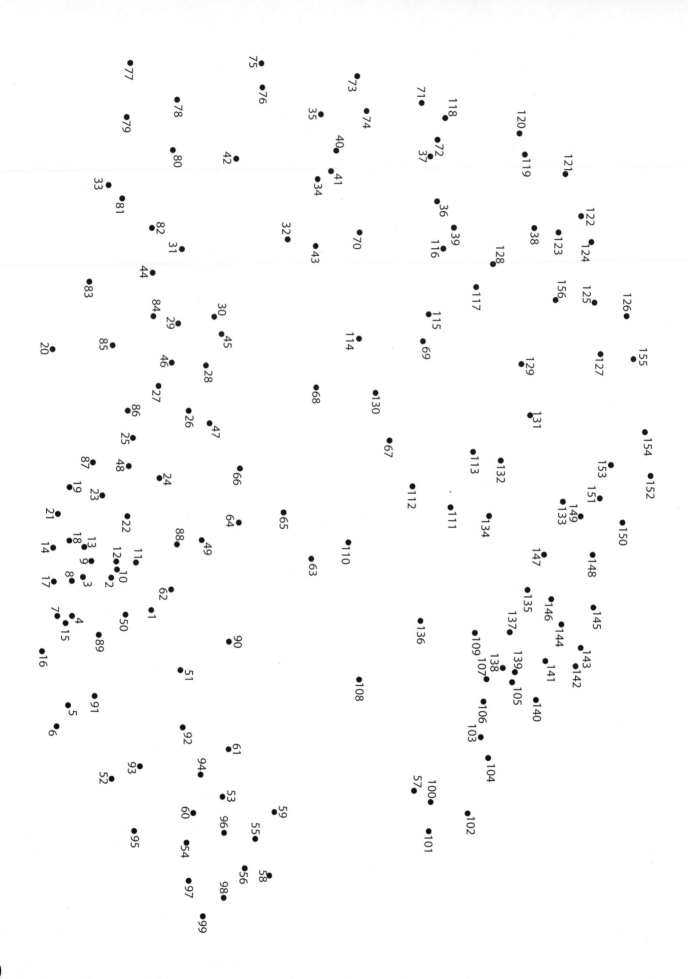

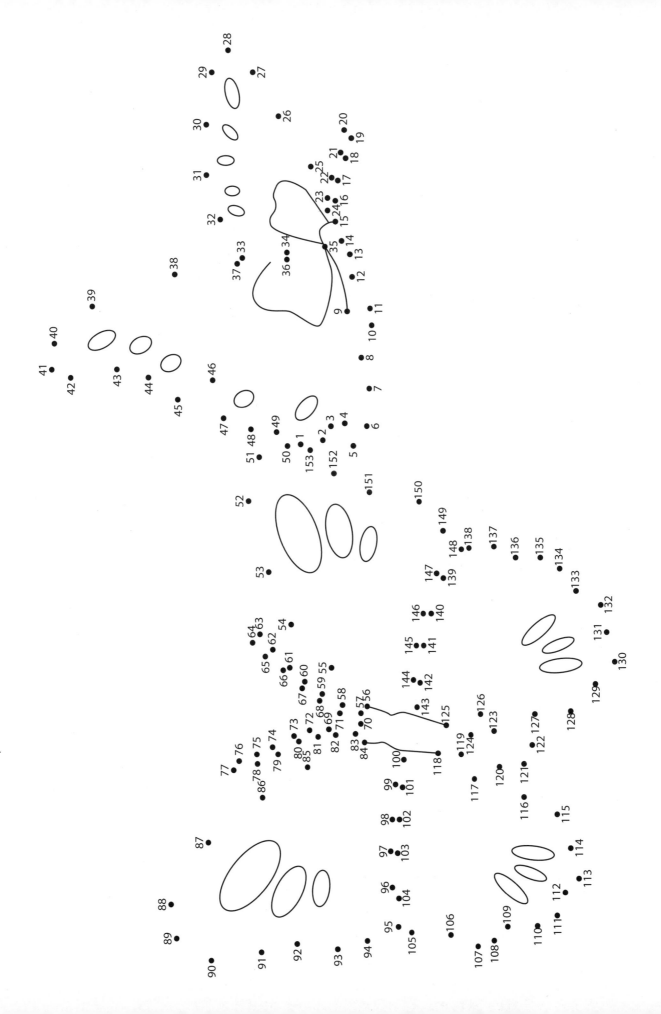

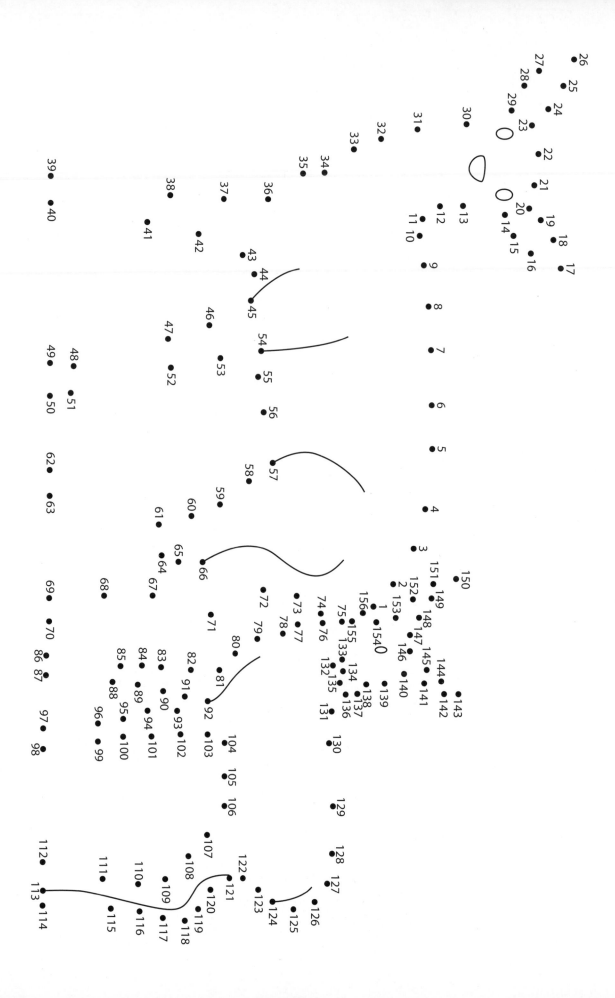

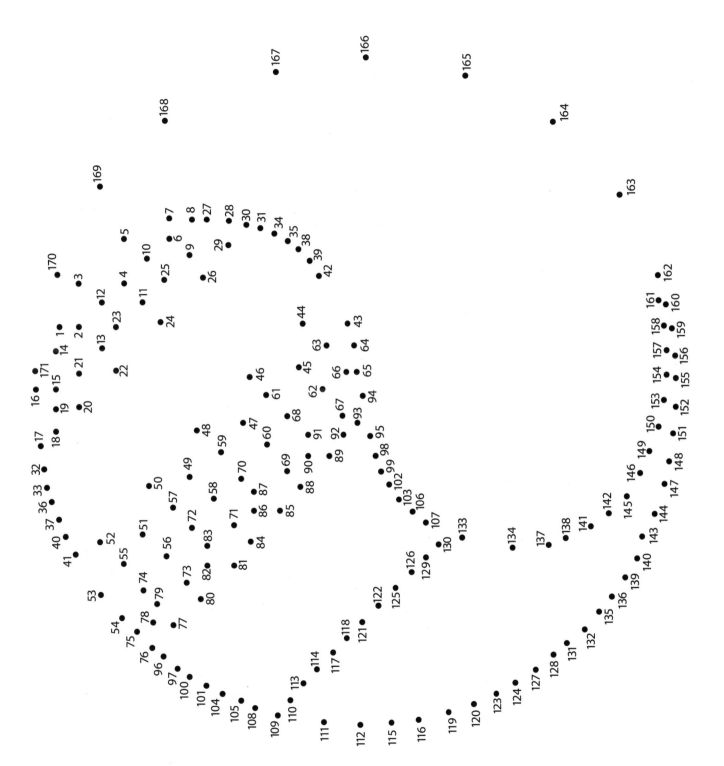

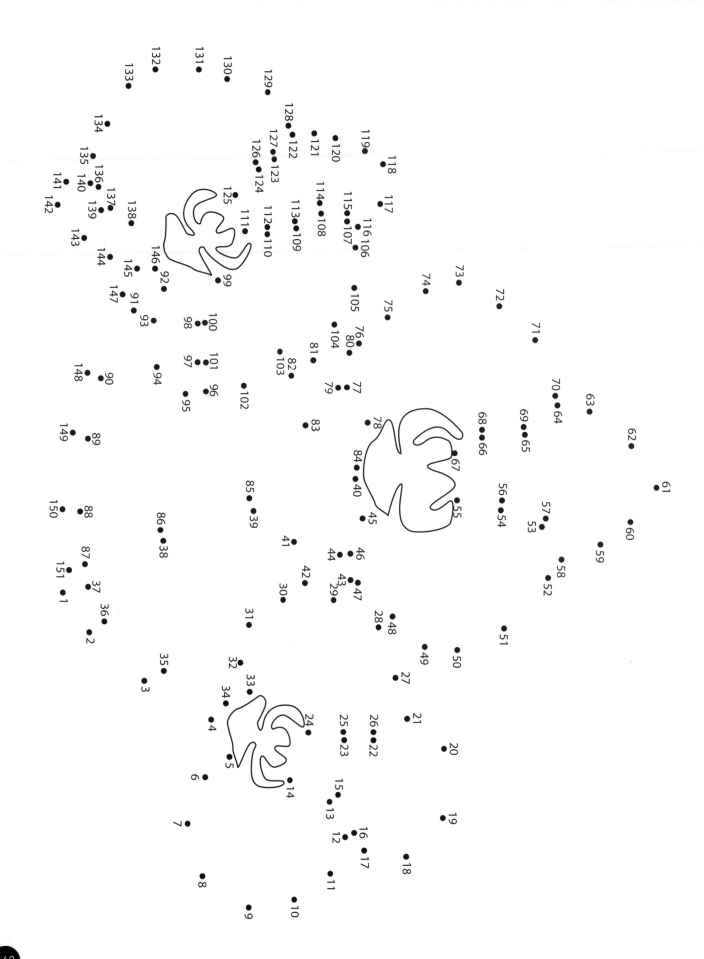

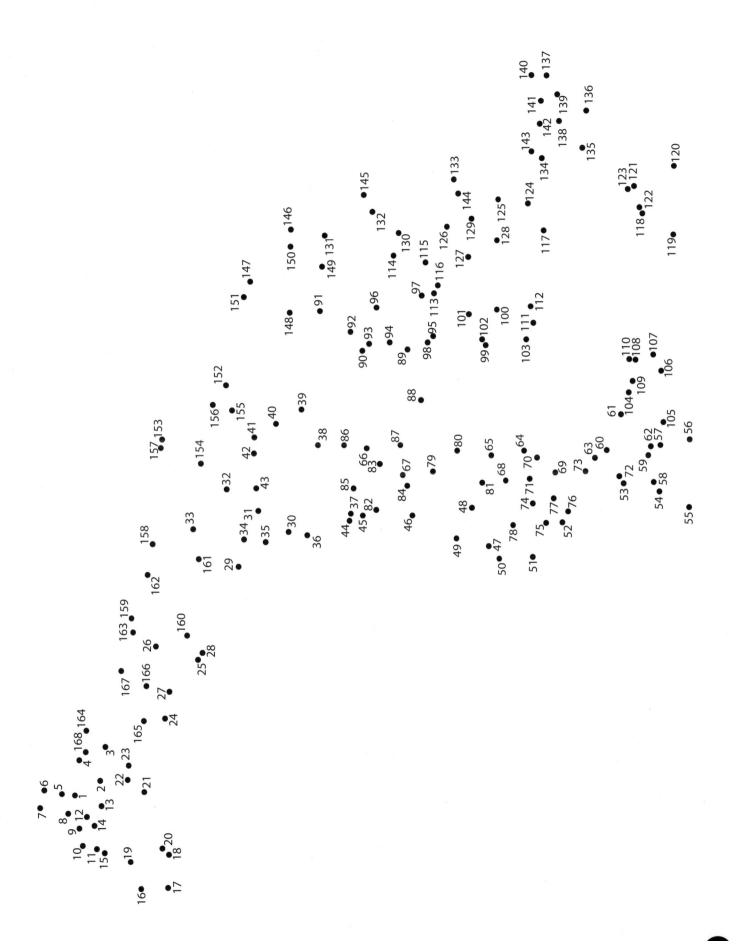

22

21

23

20

19

24
26
18

27
17

48
25
16
10
9
8
7

47
29
15
6
28
45
30
11
5
49
53
50
44
31
14
12
133
134
135
4
51
33
13
134
135
52
43
32
37
136
3
54
56
34
132
137
2
55
59
42
35
1
57
38
58
60
36
40
131
61
39
62
41
130
63
129
64
114
128
115
65
127
121
120
116
113
122
111
112
66
126
123
119
117
110
75
124
74
76
118
109
108
107
95
94
125
73
105
106
103
96
72
100
101
104
97
93
77
102
98
92
99
90
91
67
71
78
89
79
88
68
70
80
87
81
82
86
69
83
85

84

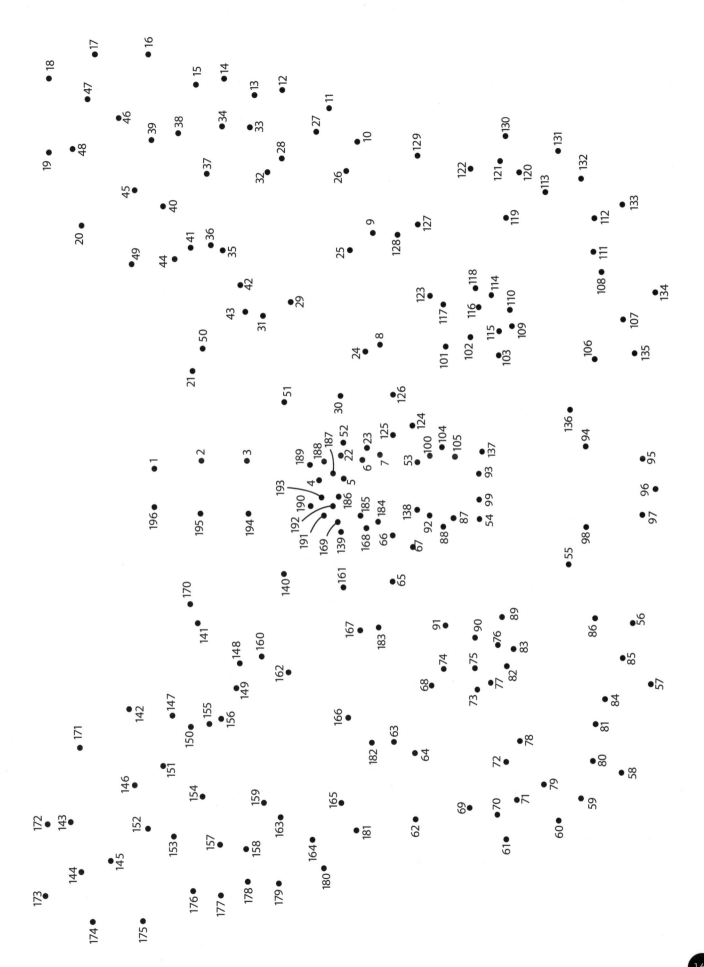

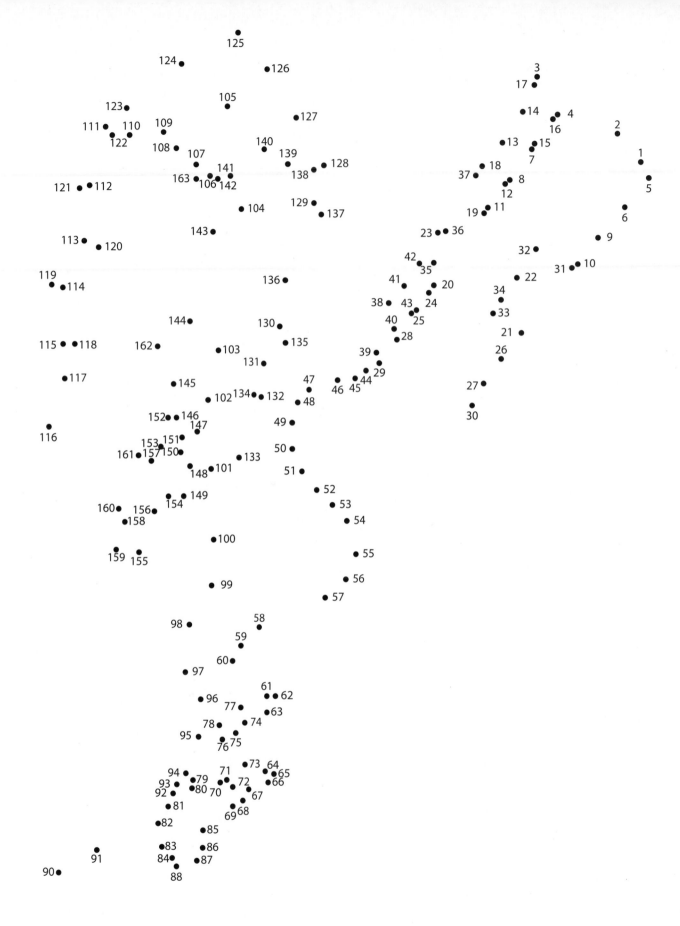

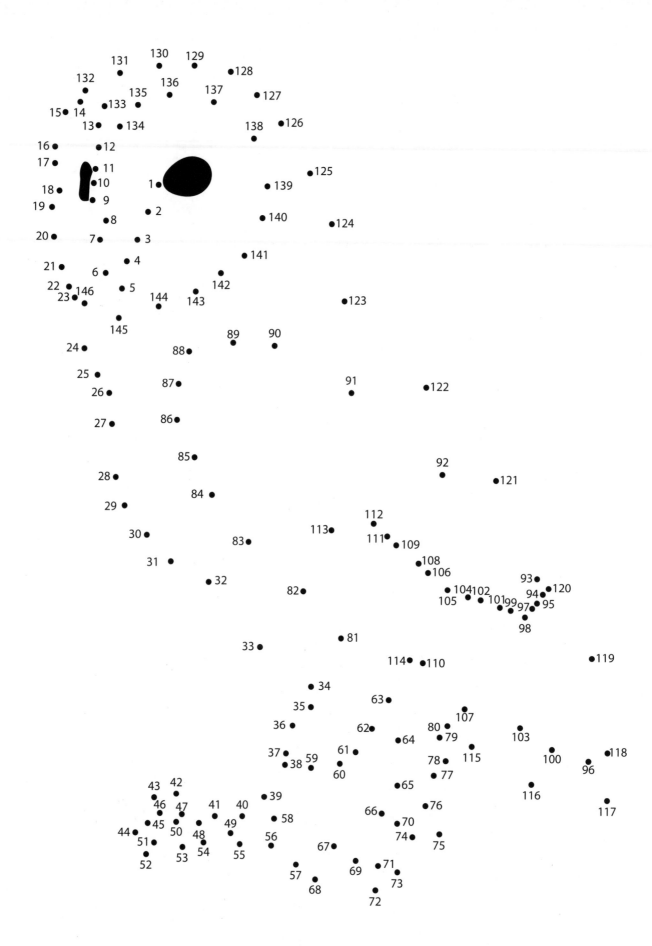

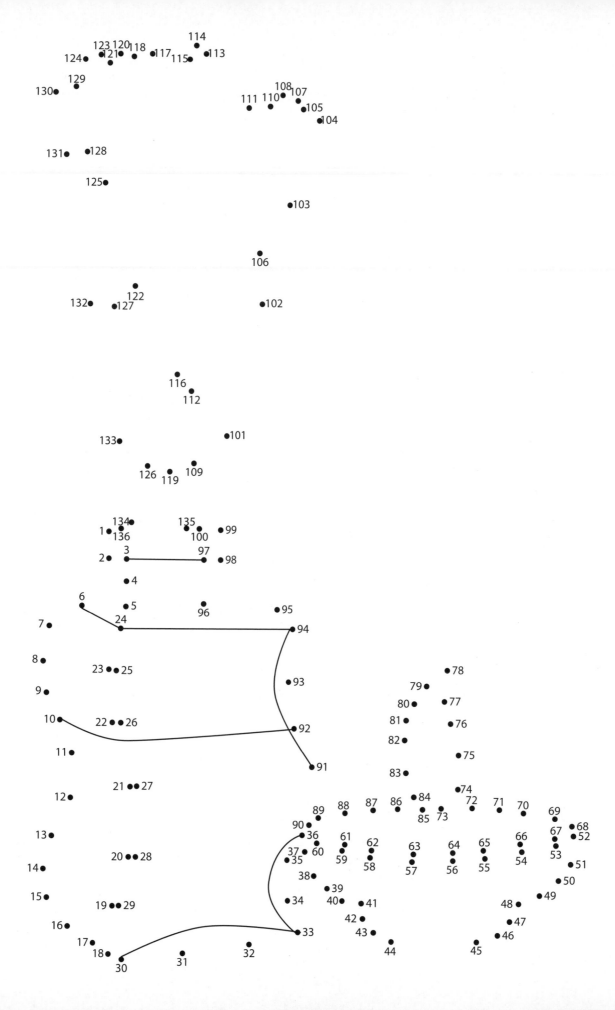

171

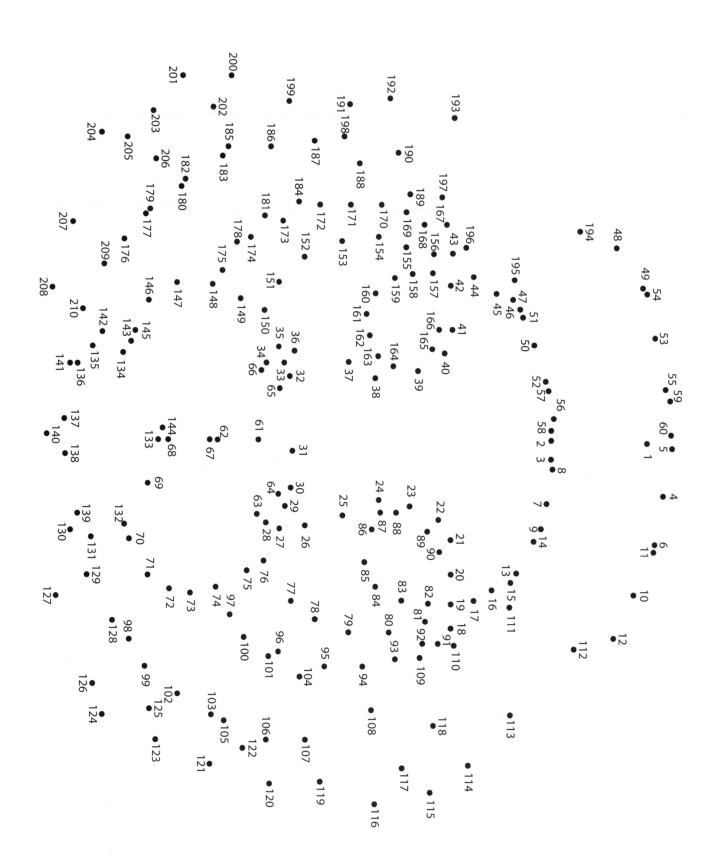

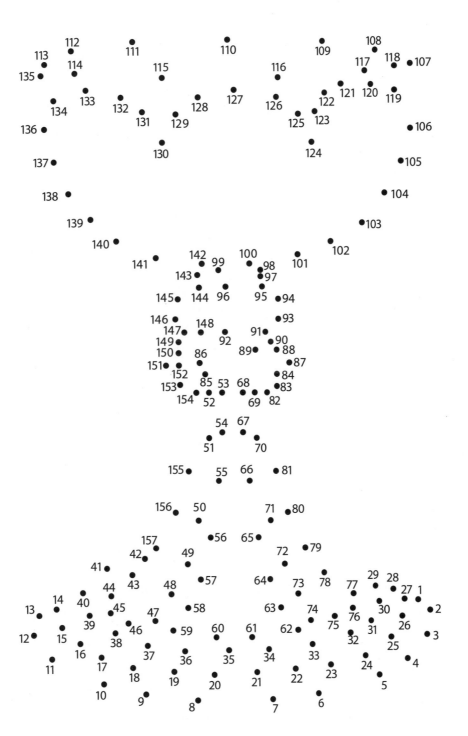

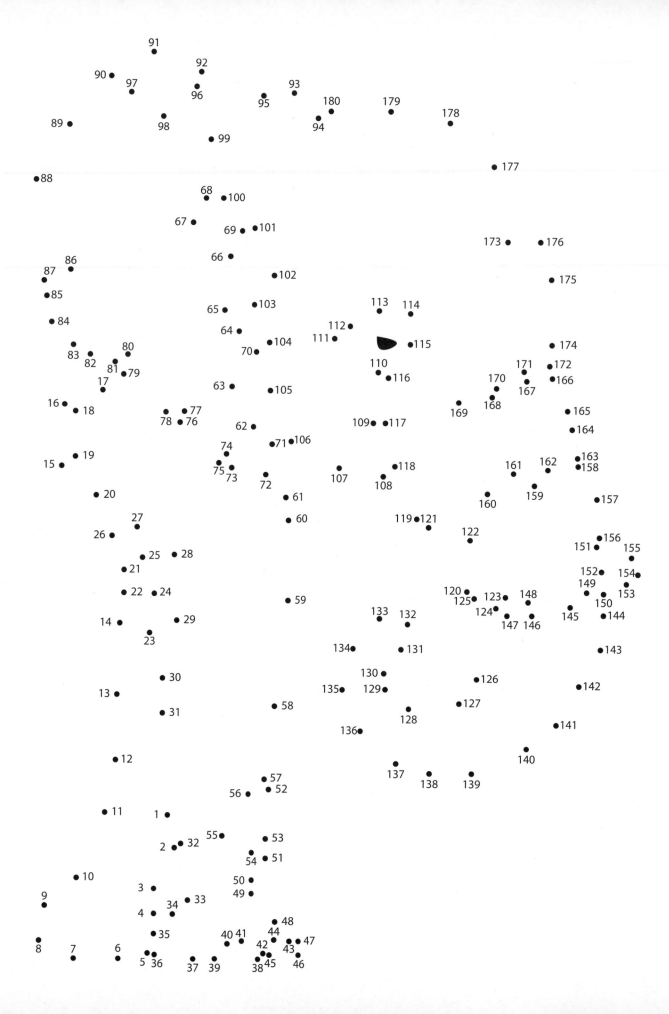

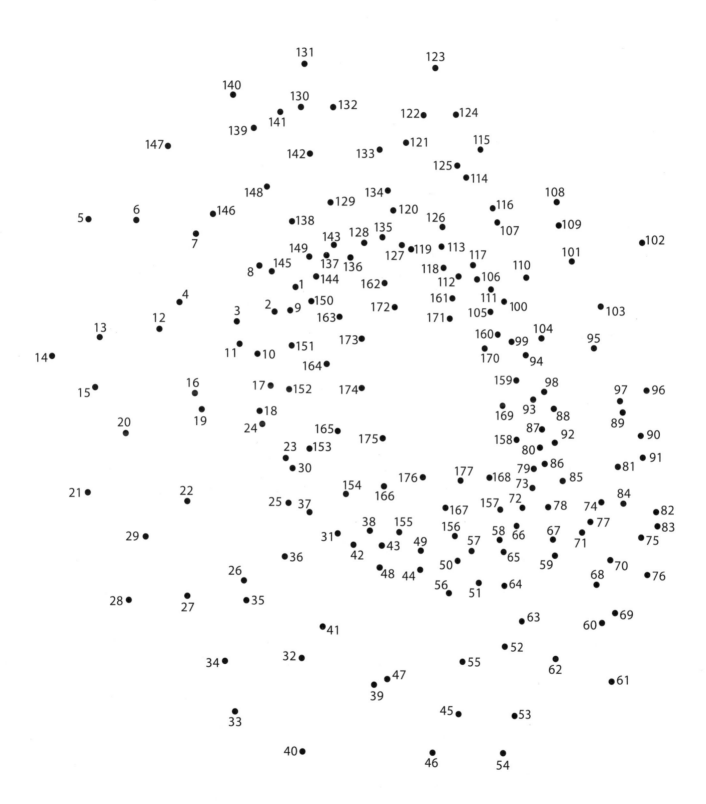

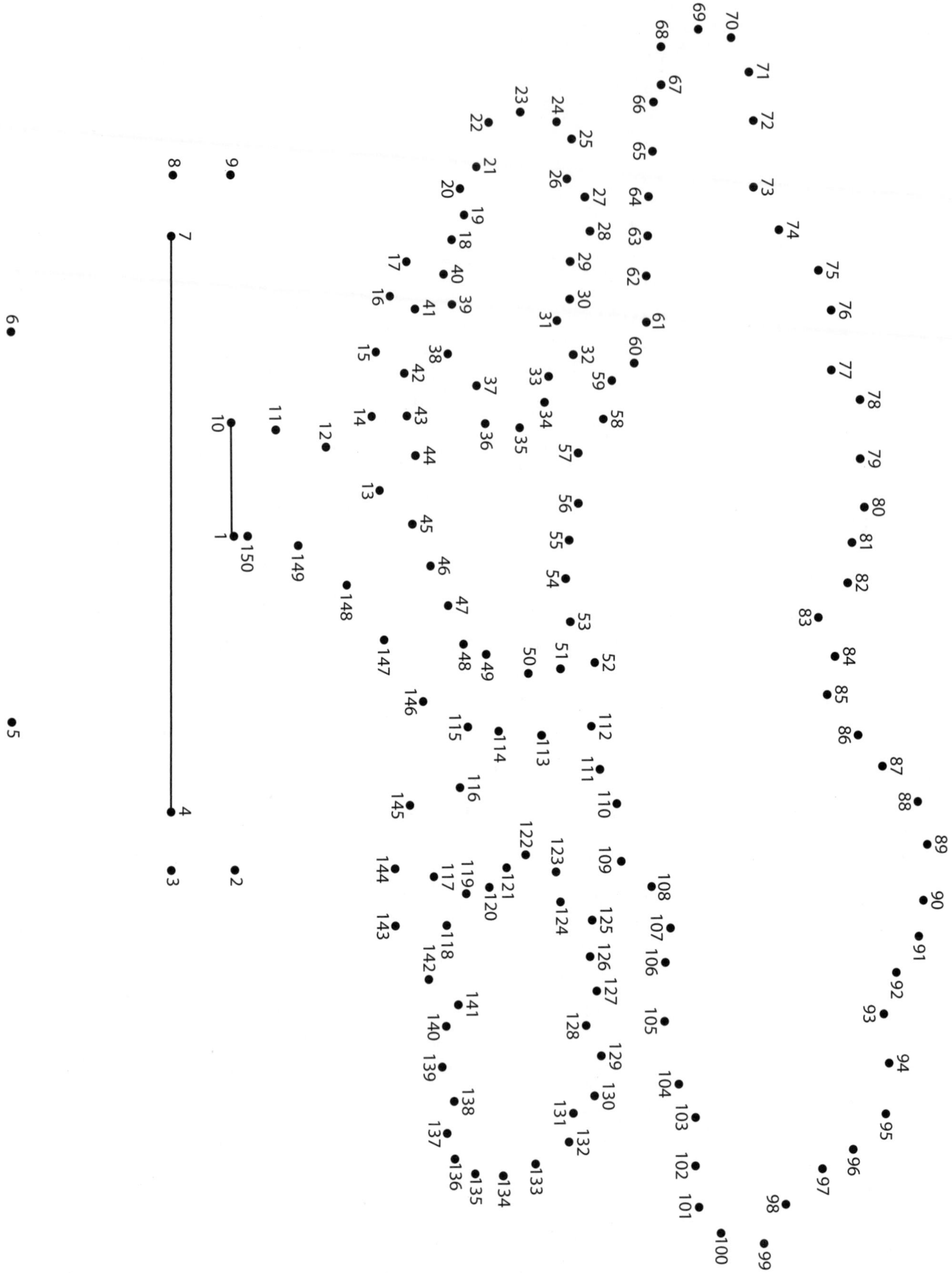

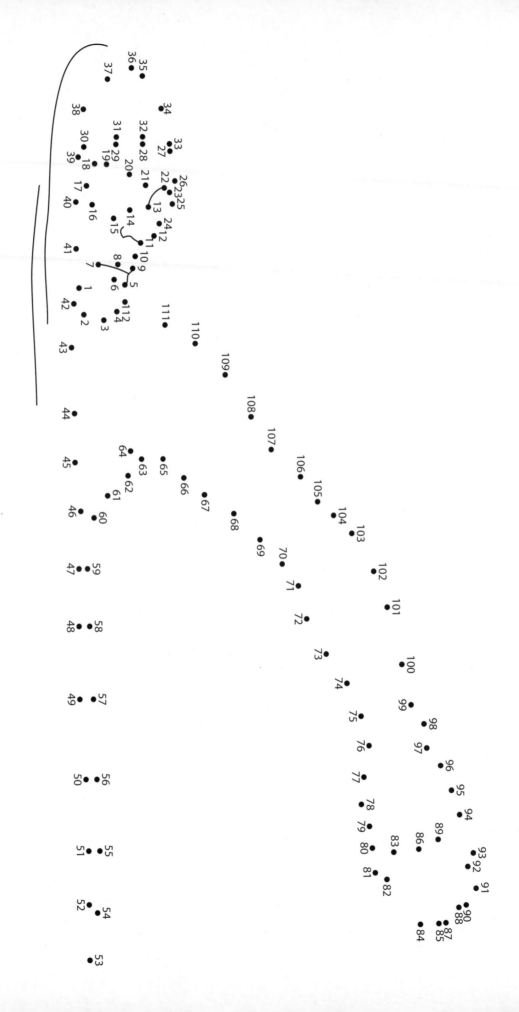

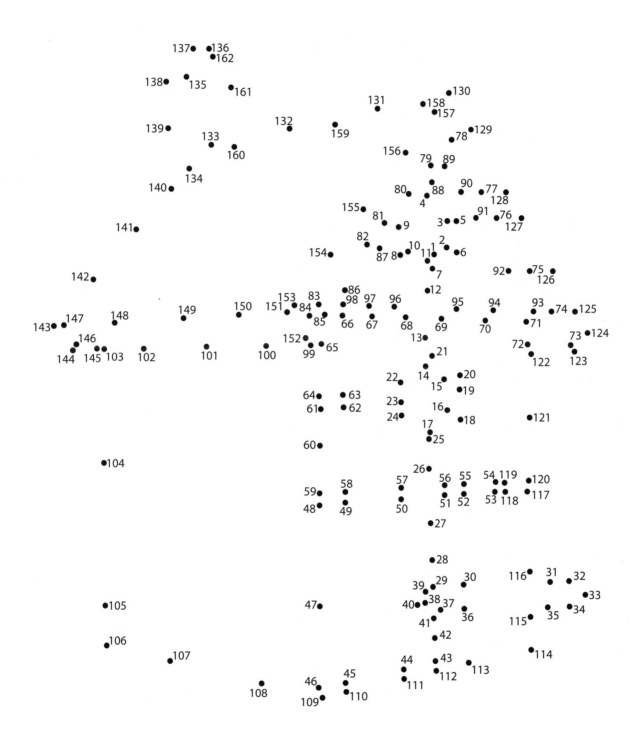

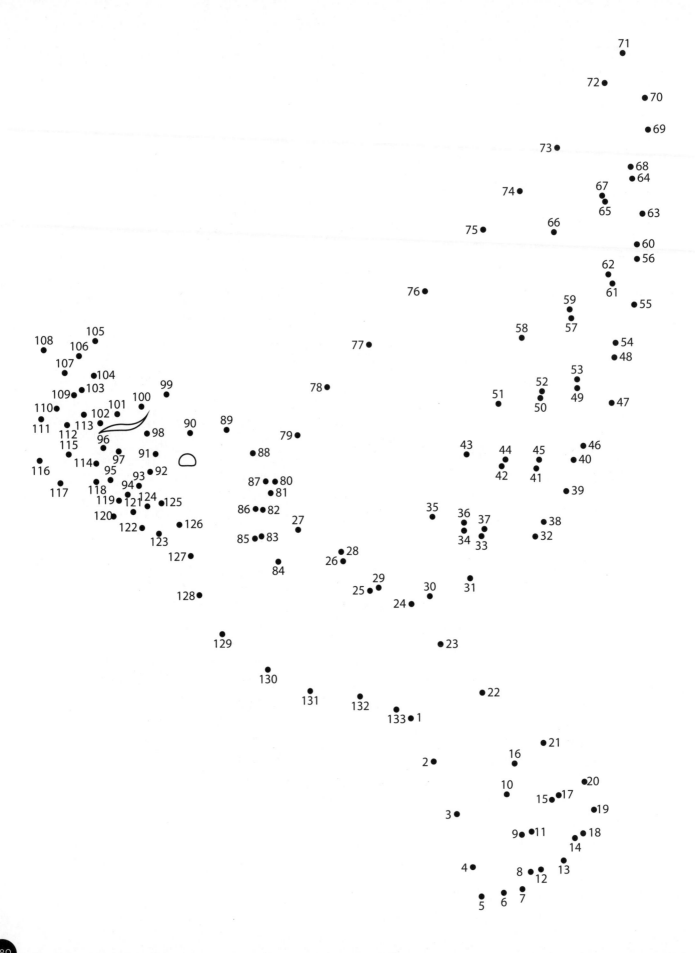

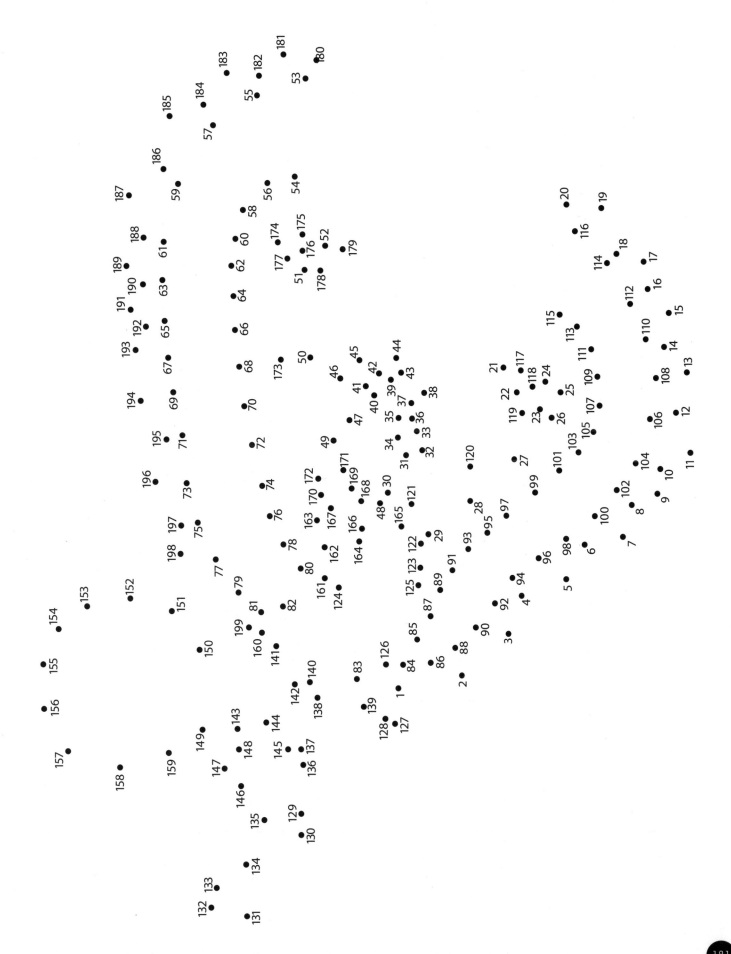

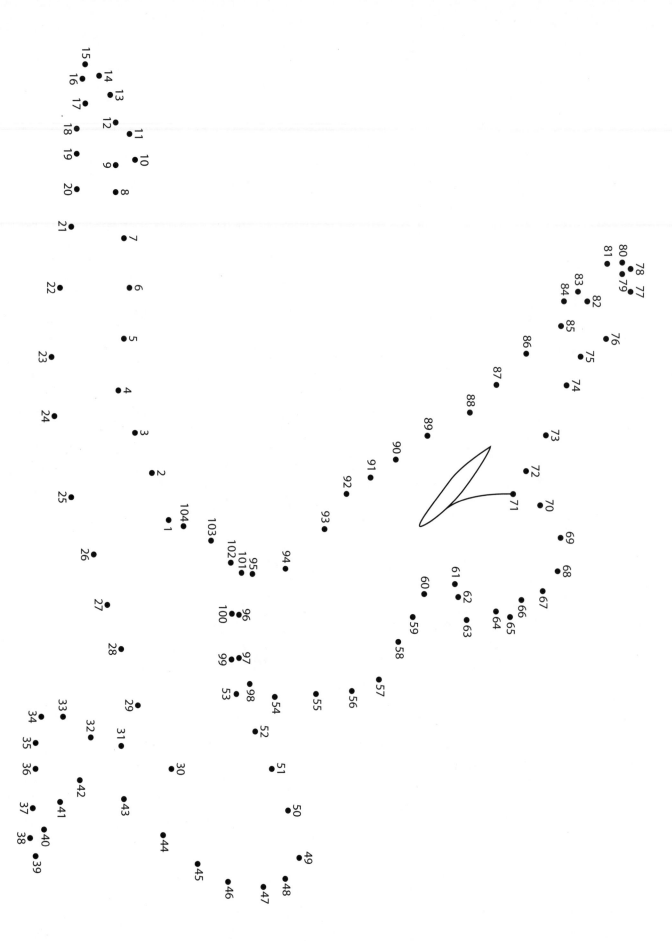

183

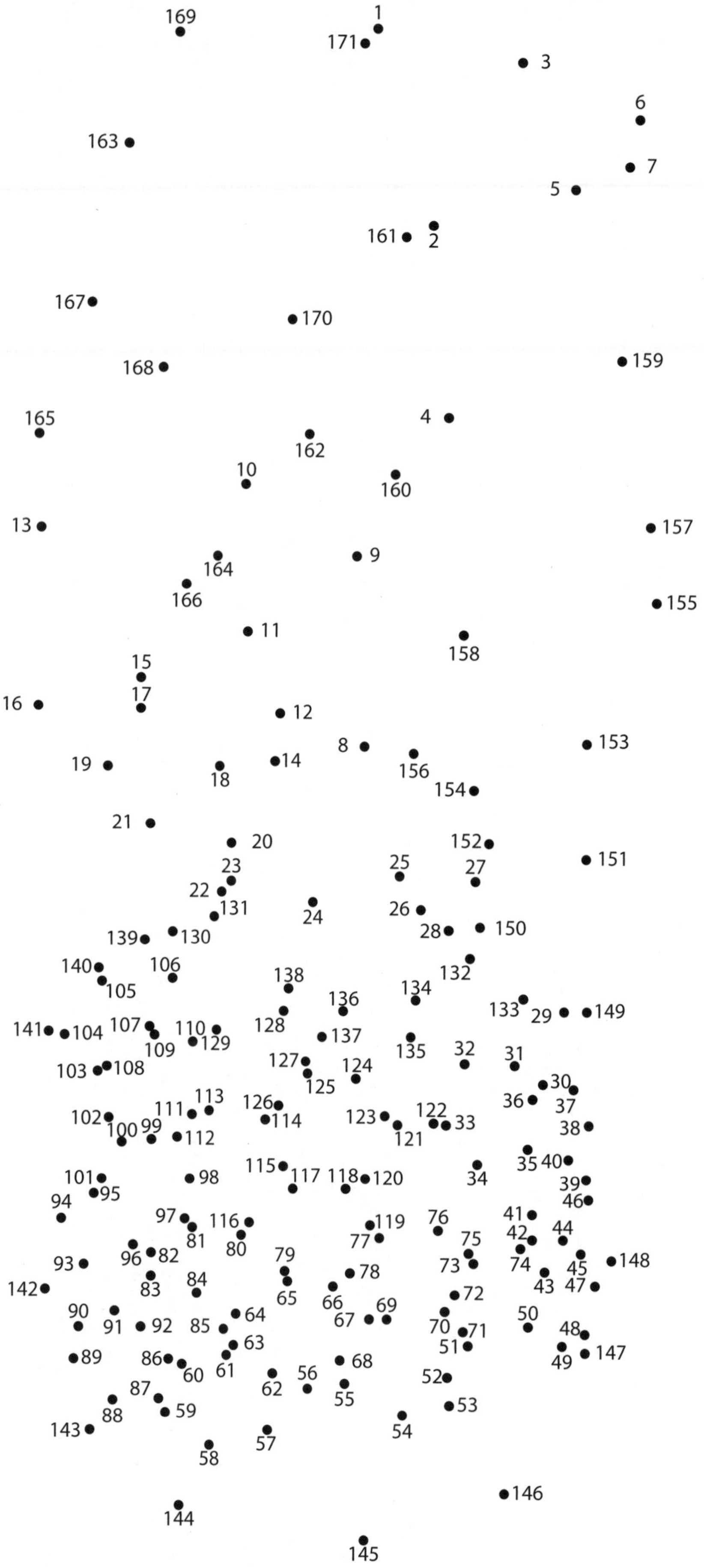

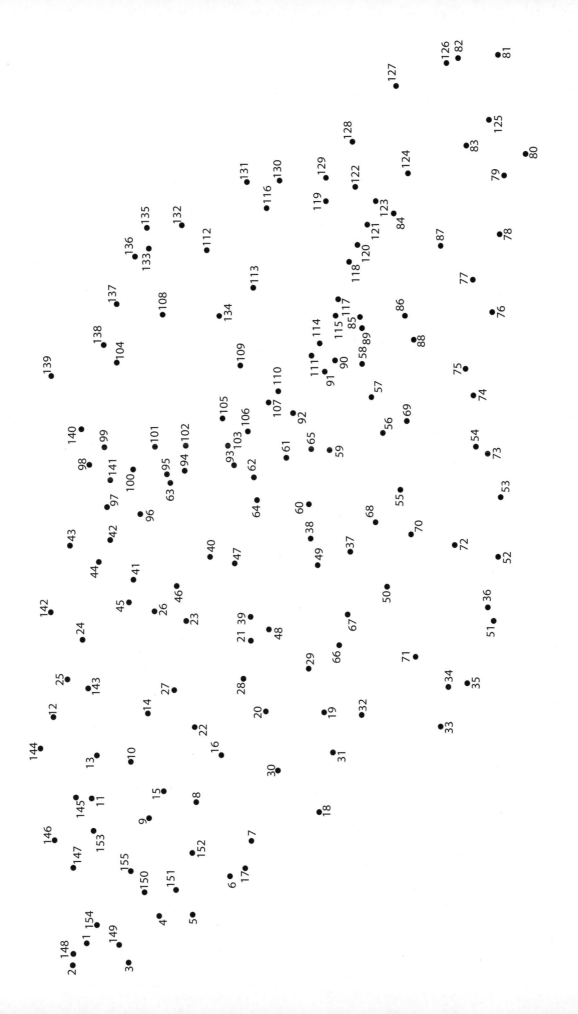

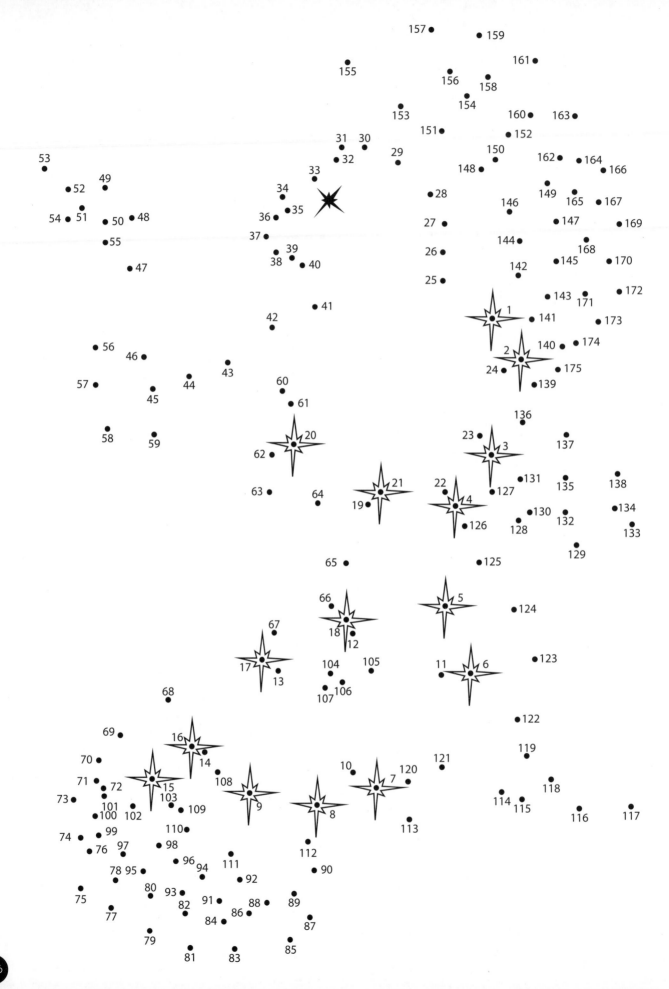

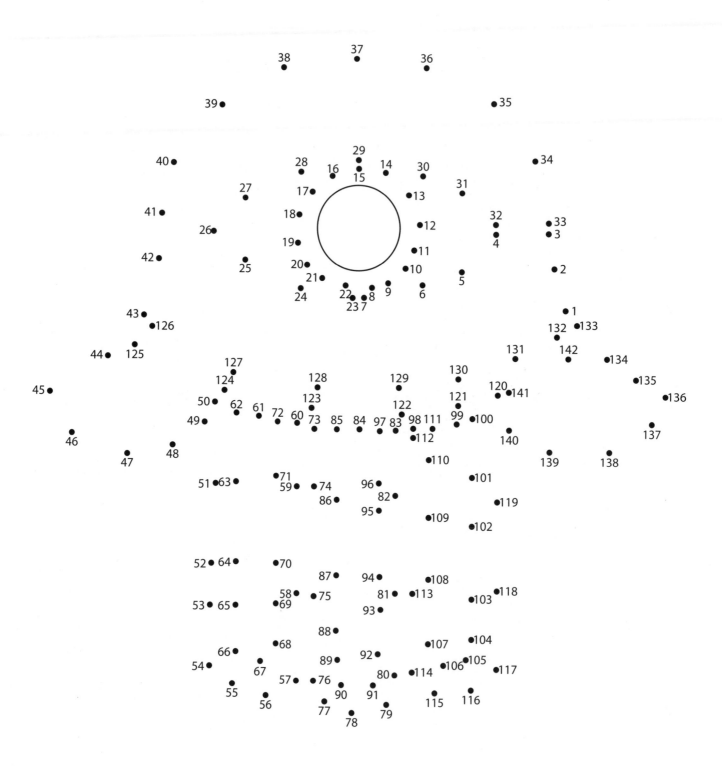

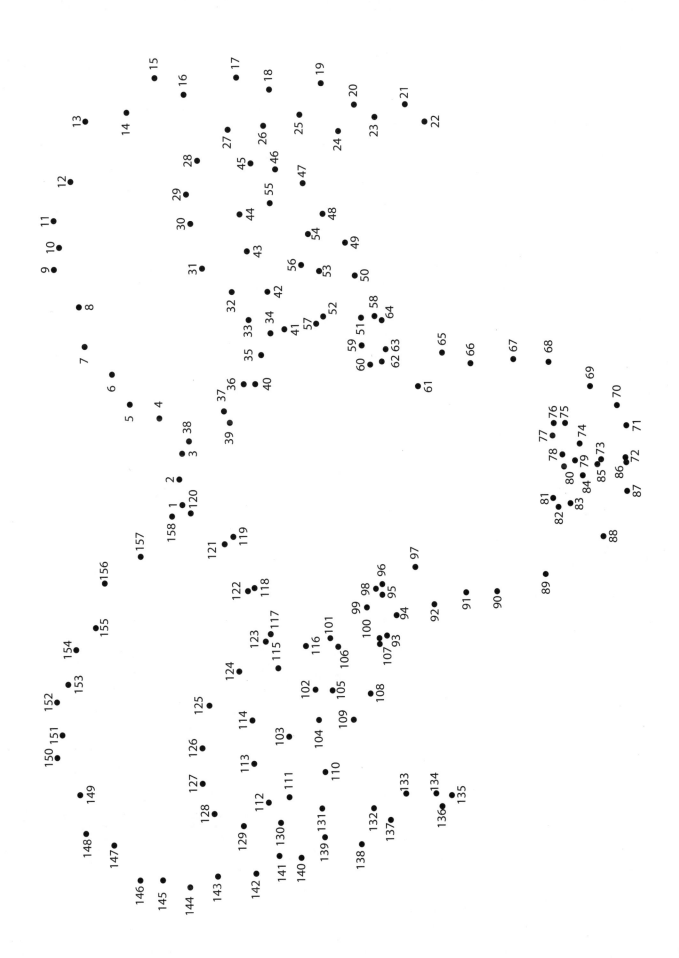

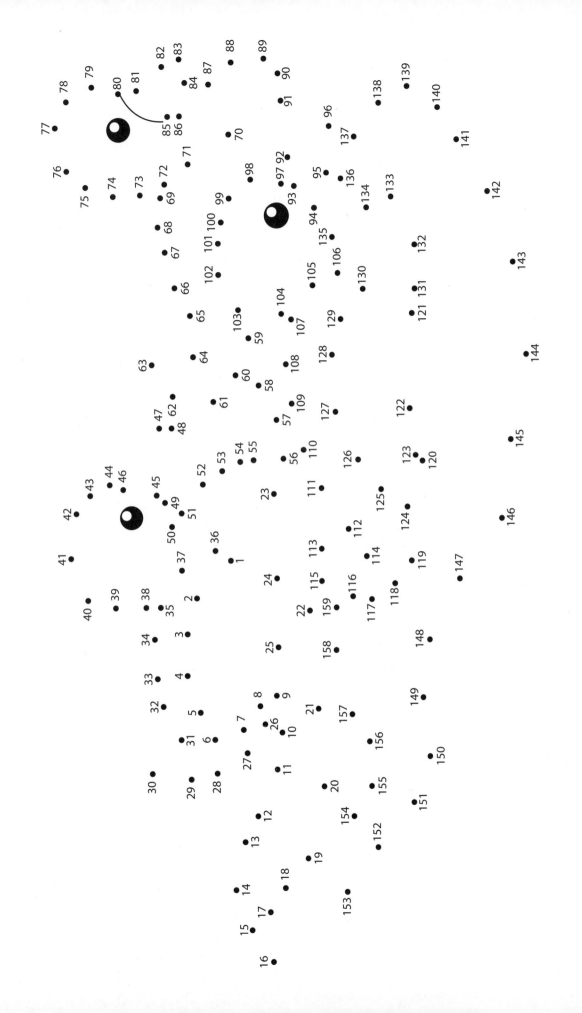

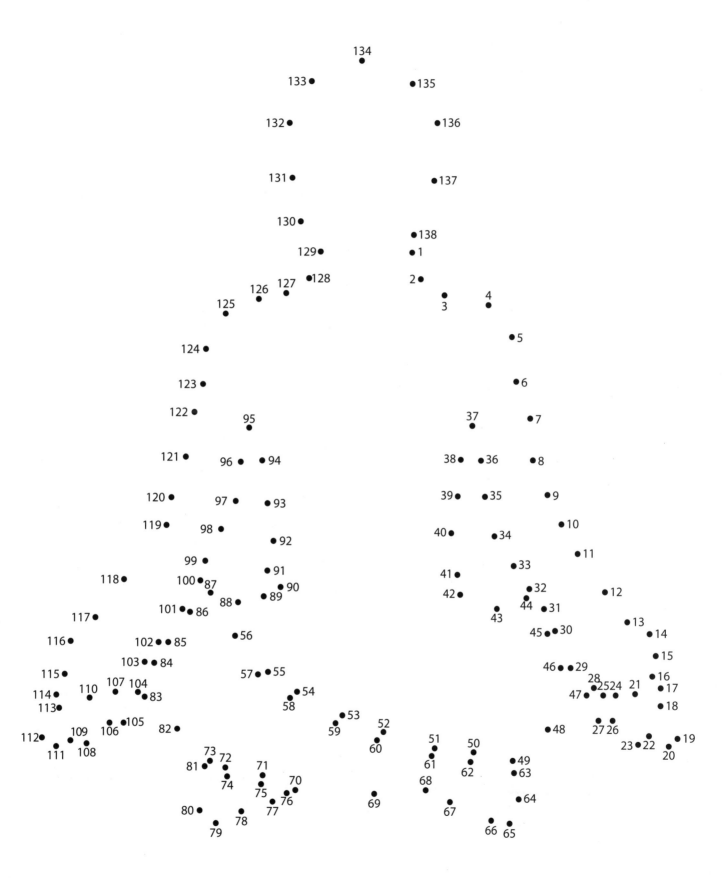

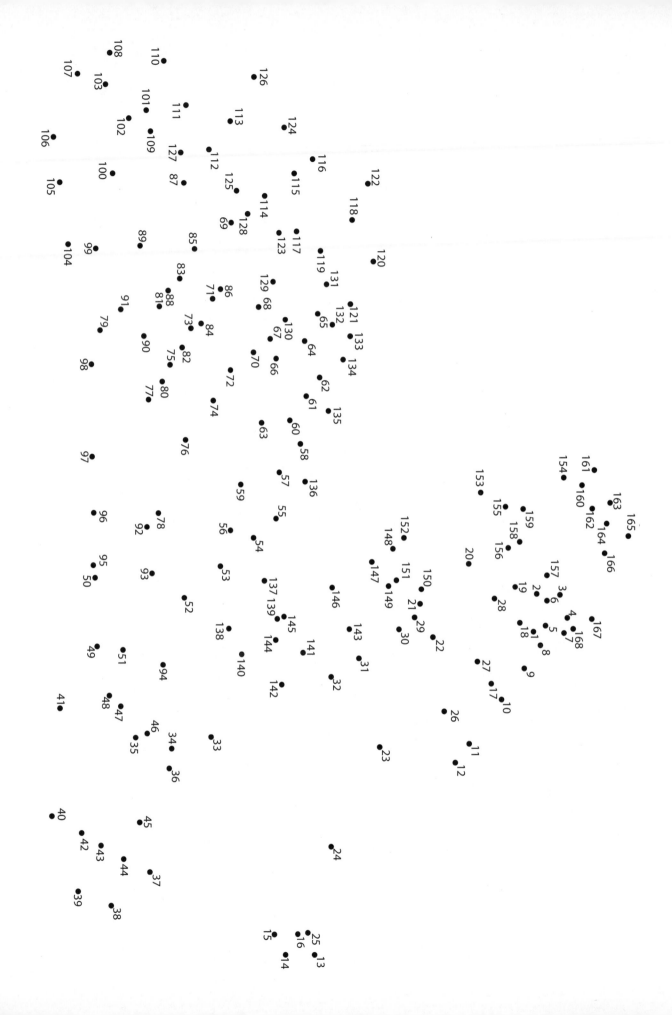

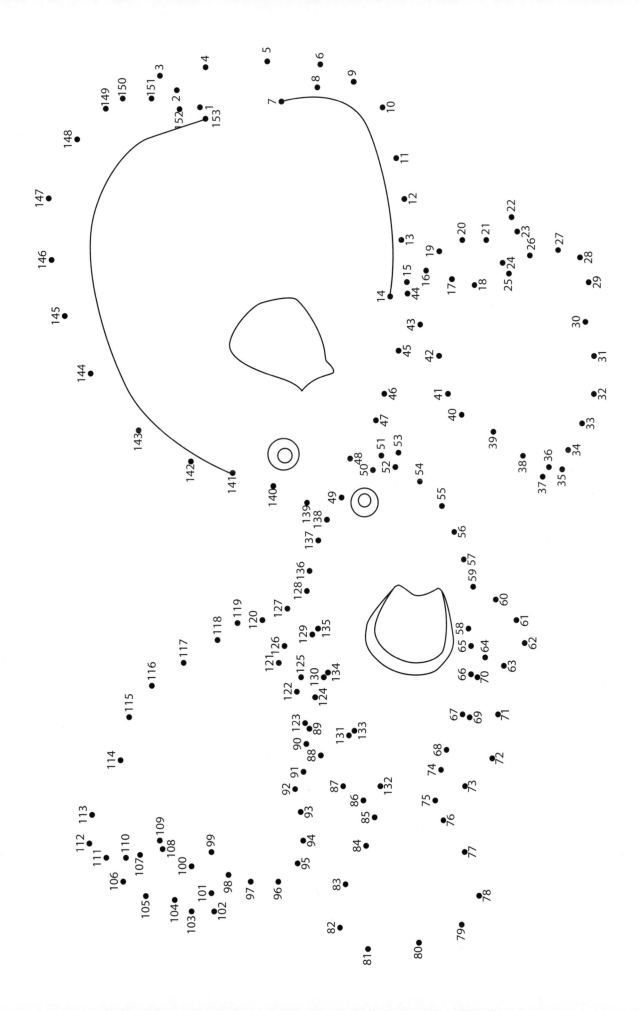

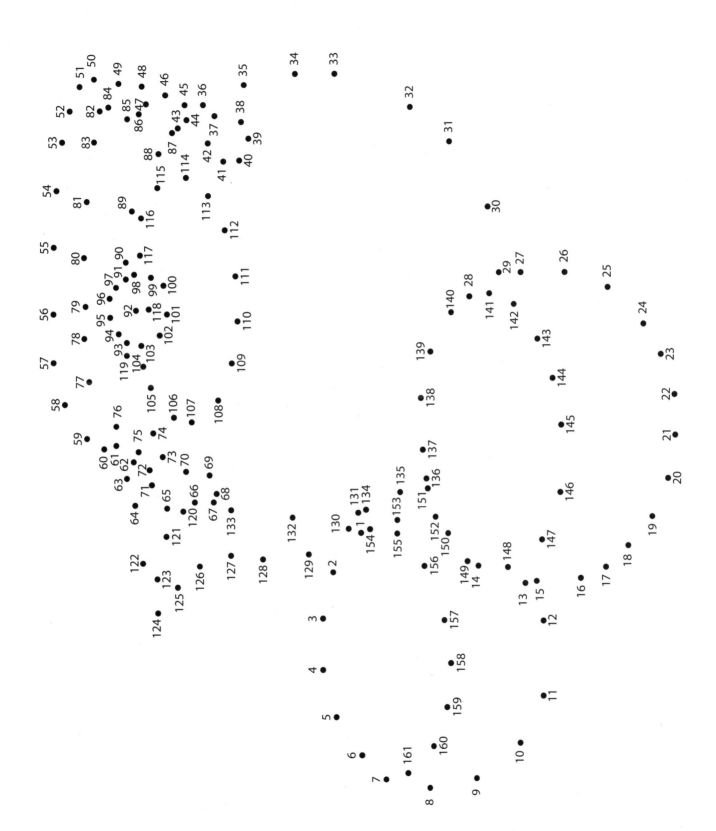

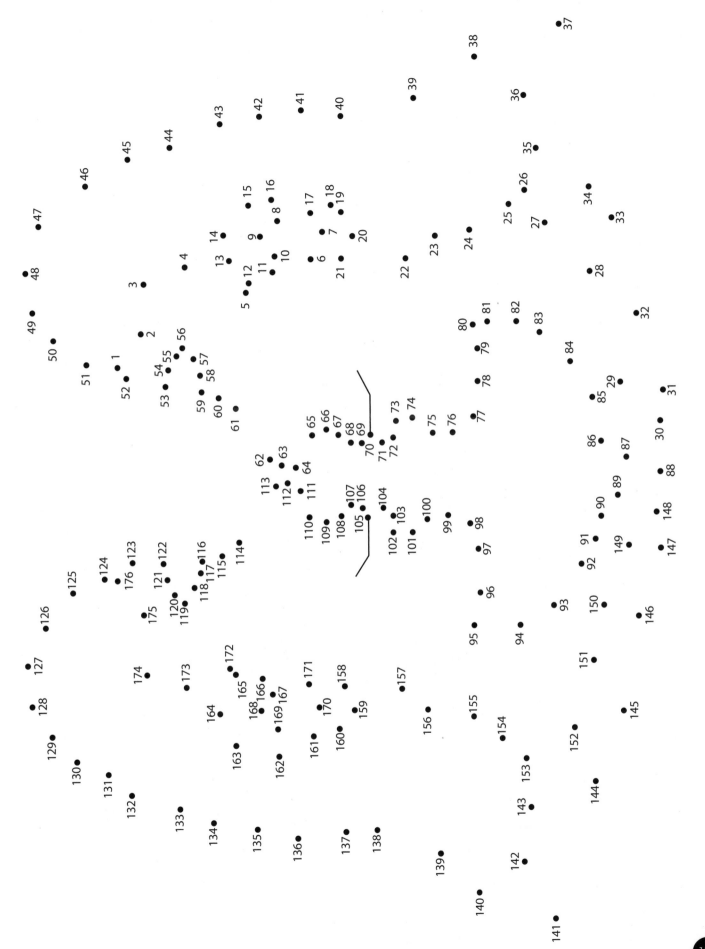

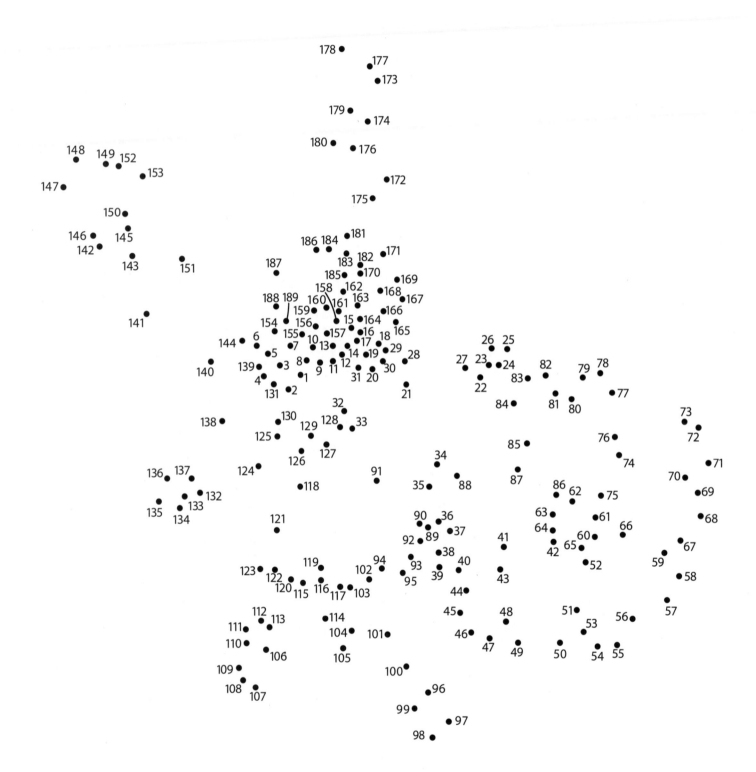

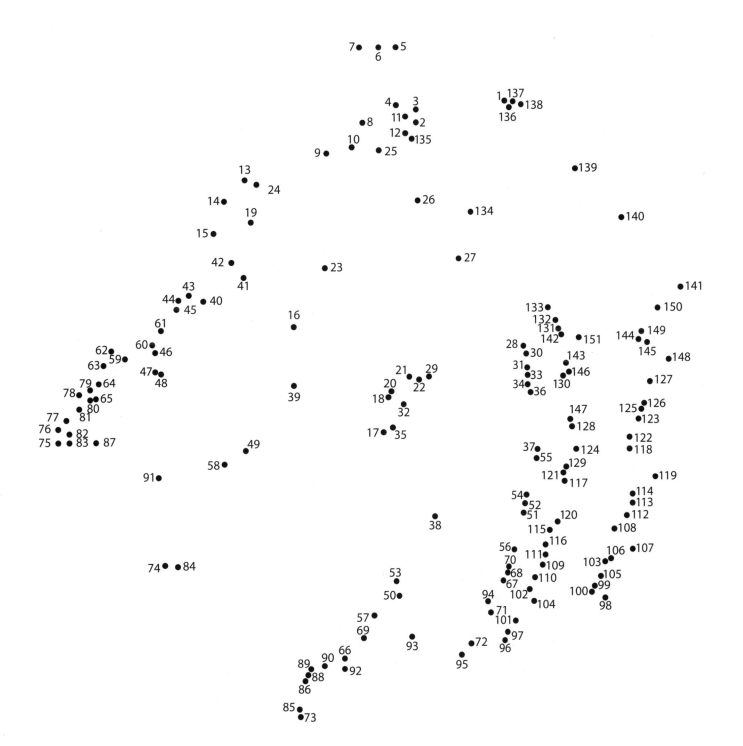

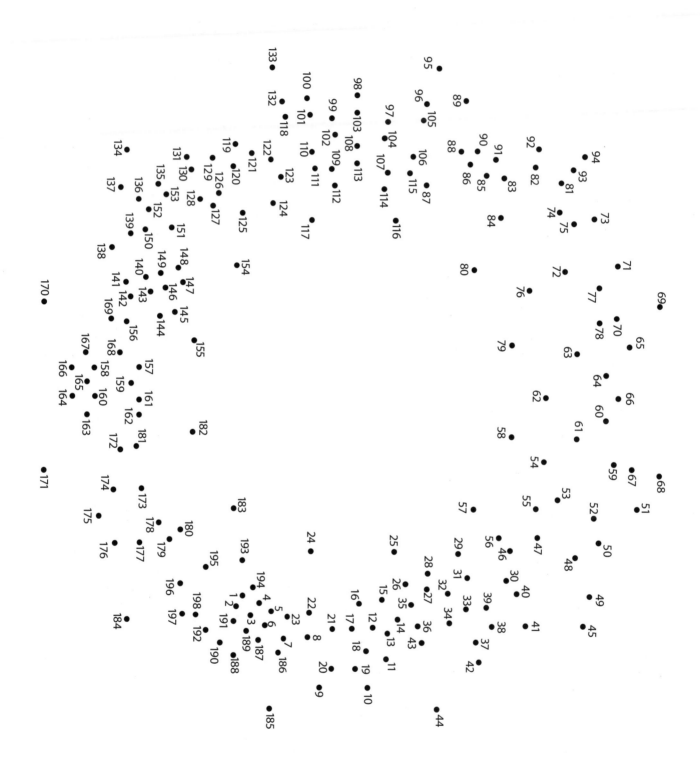

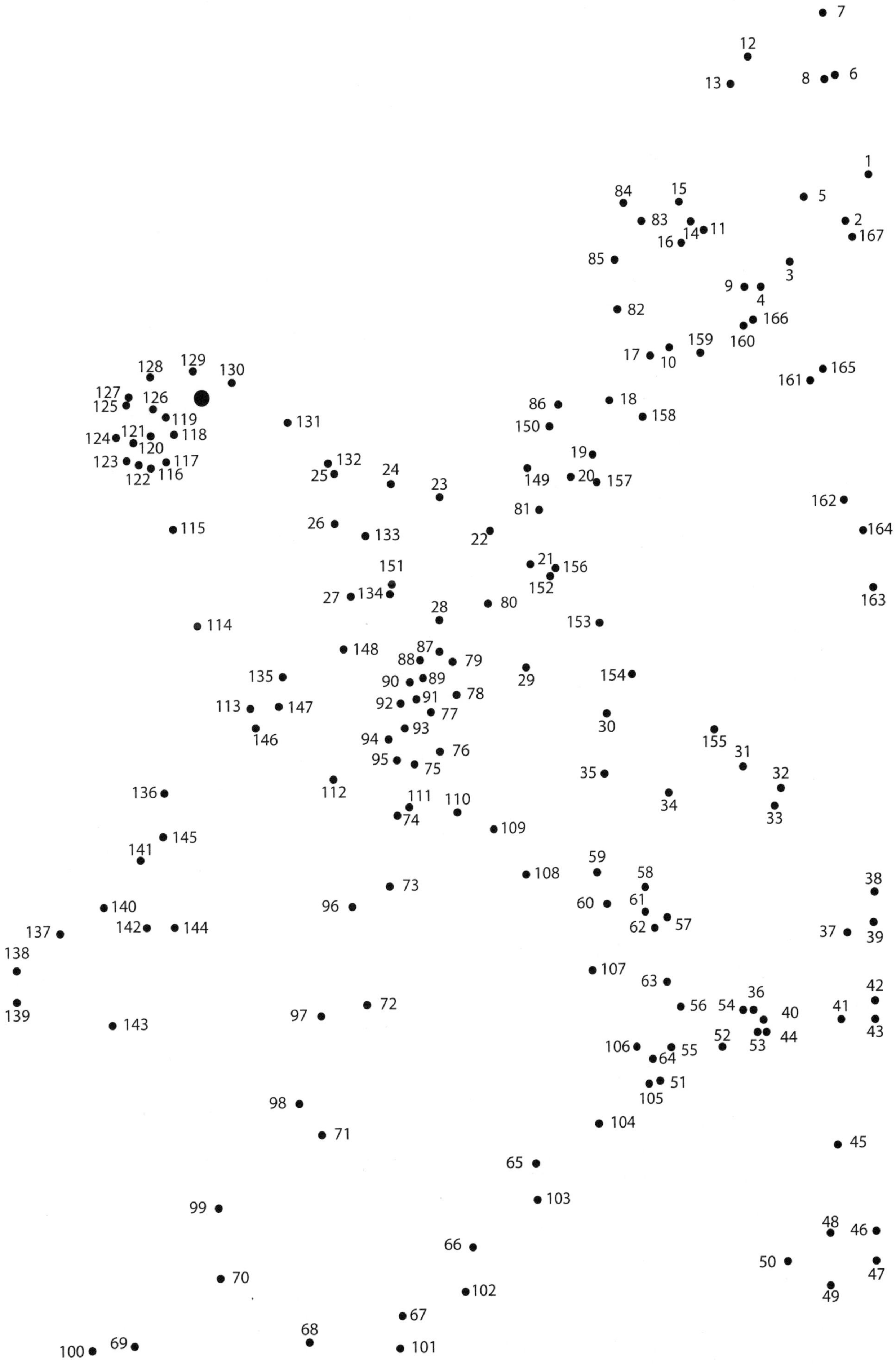

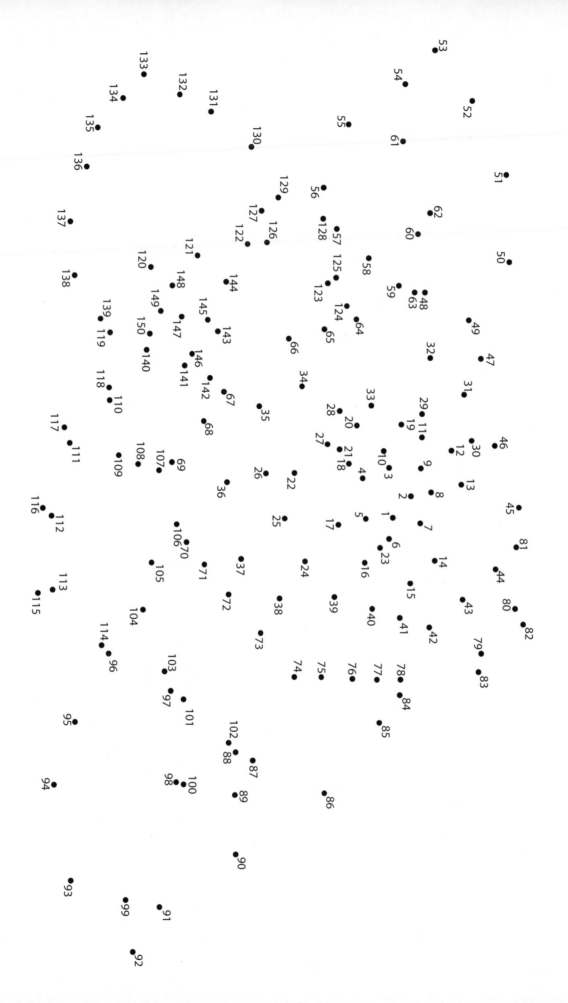

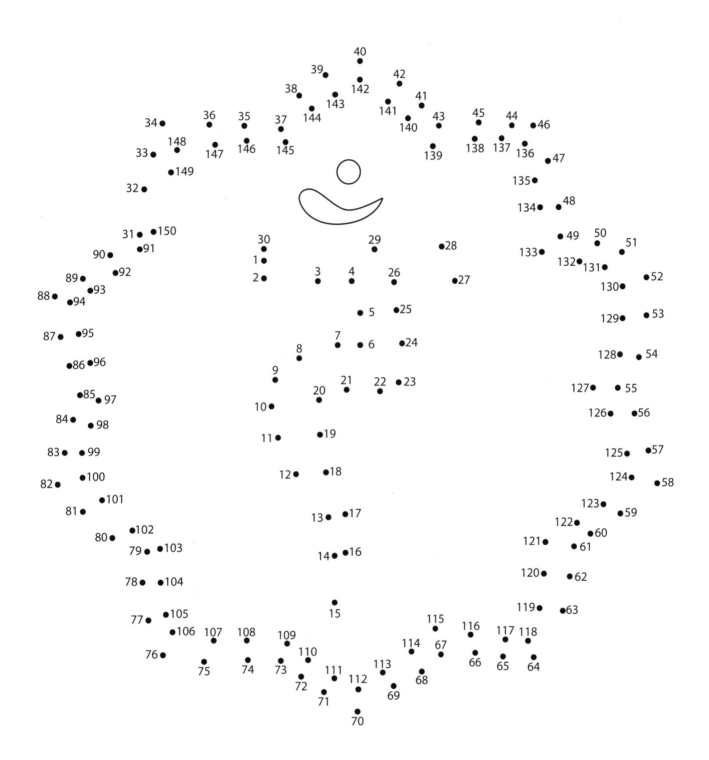

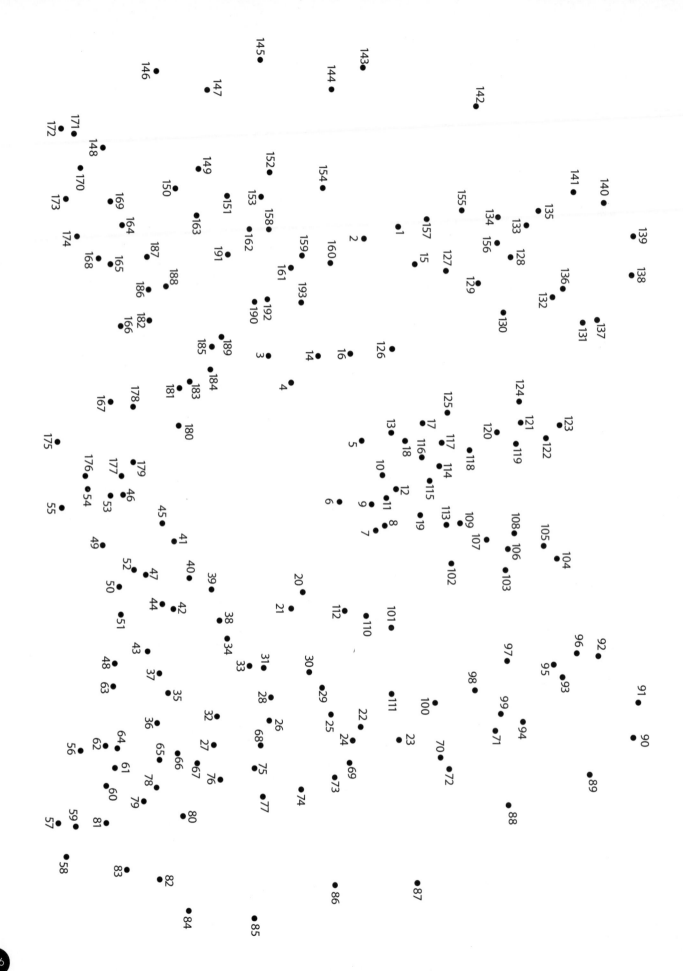

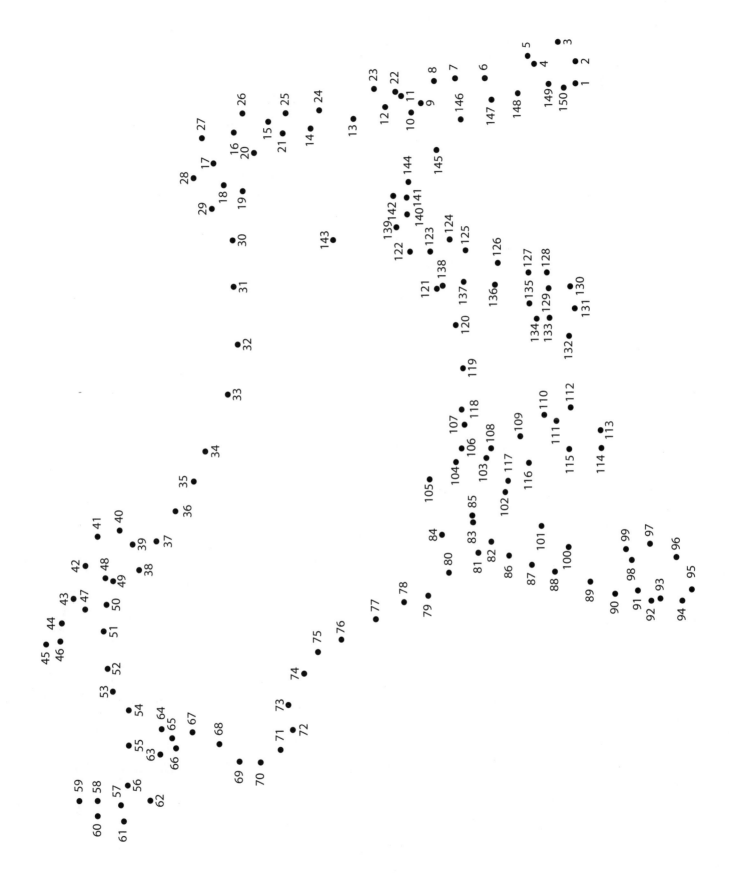

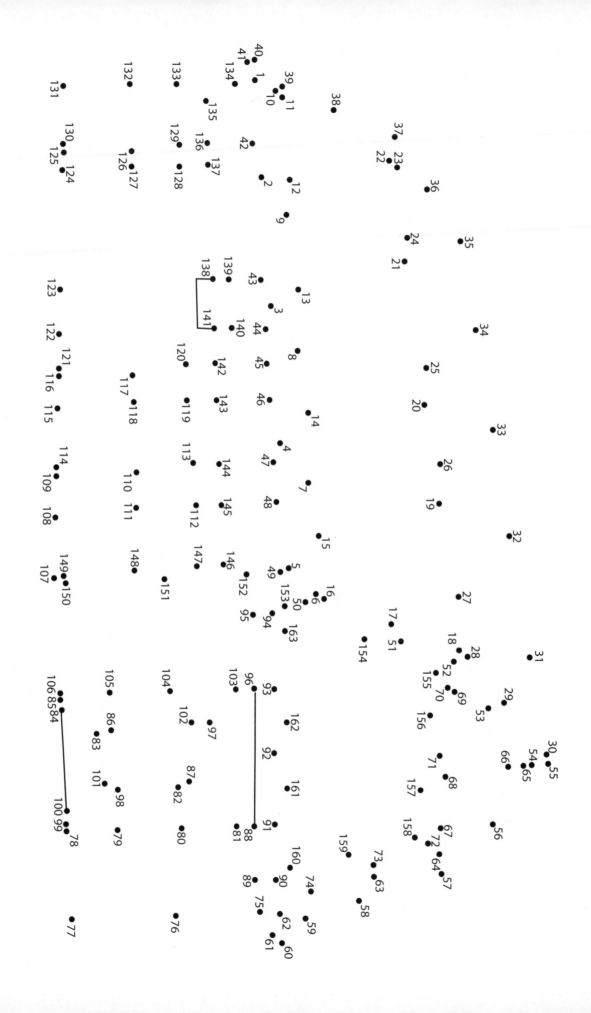

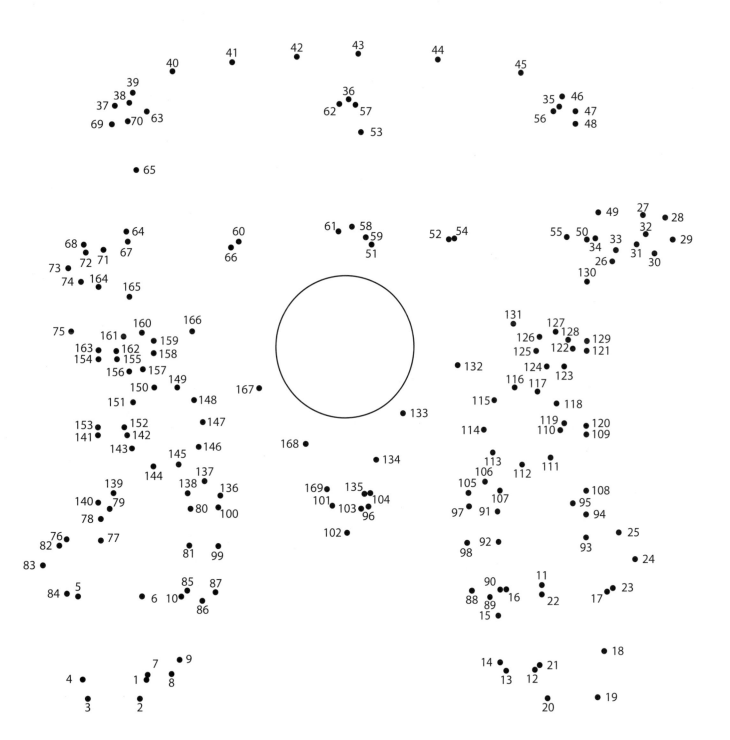

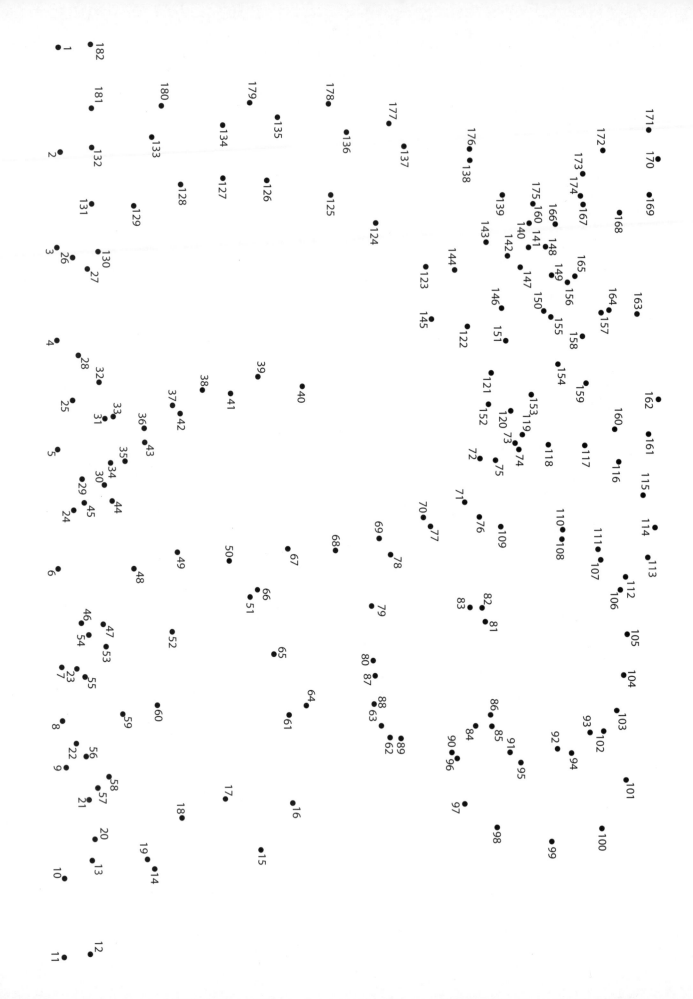

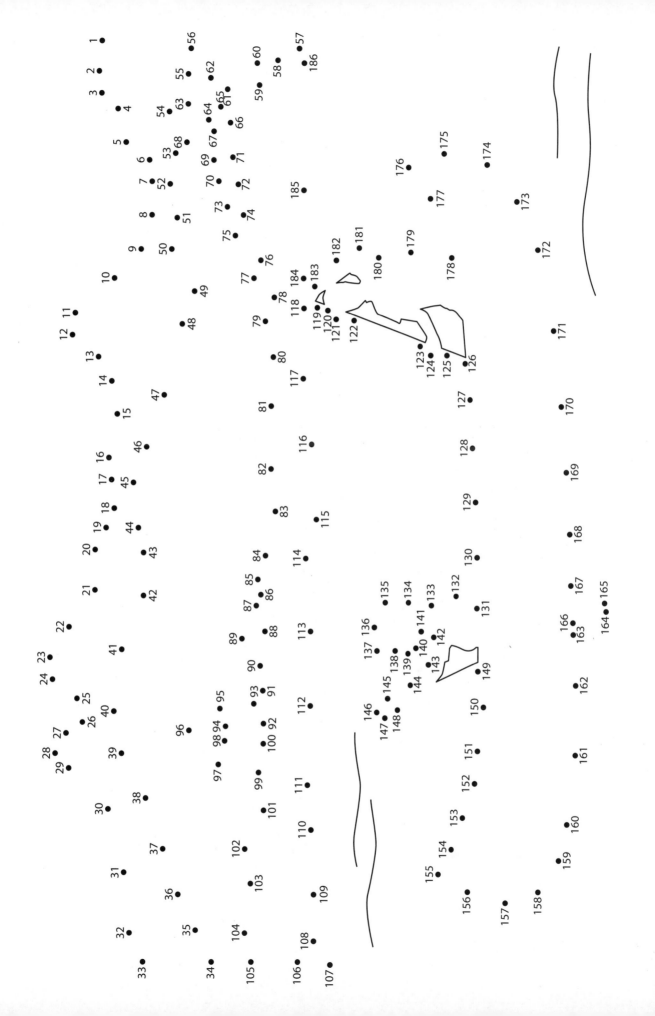

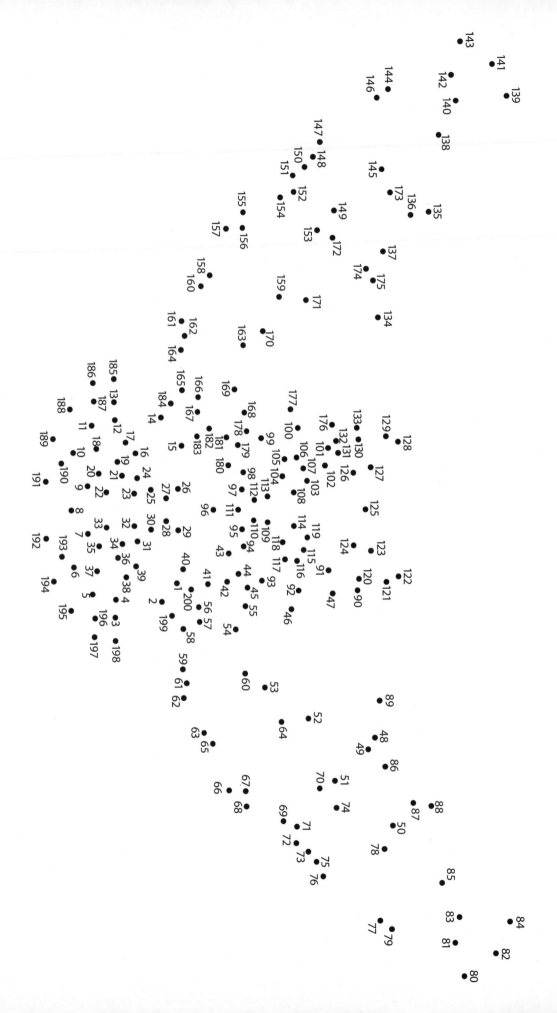

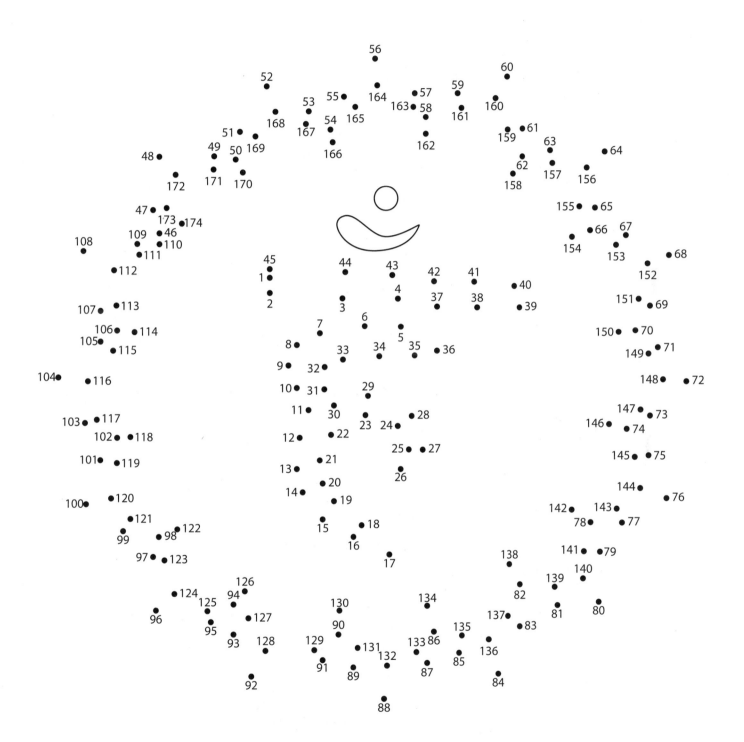

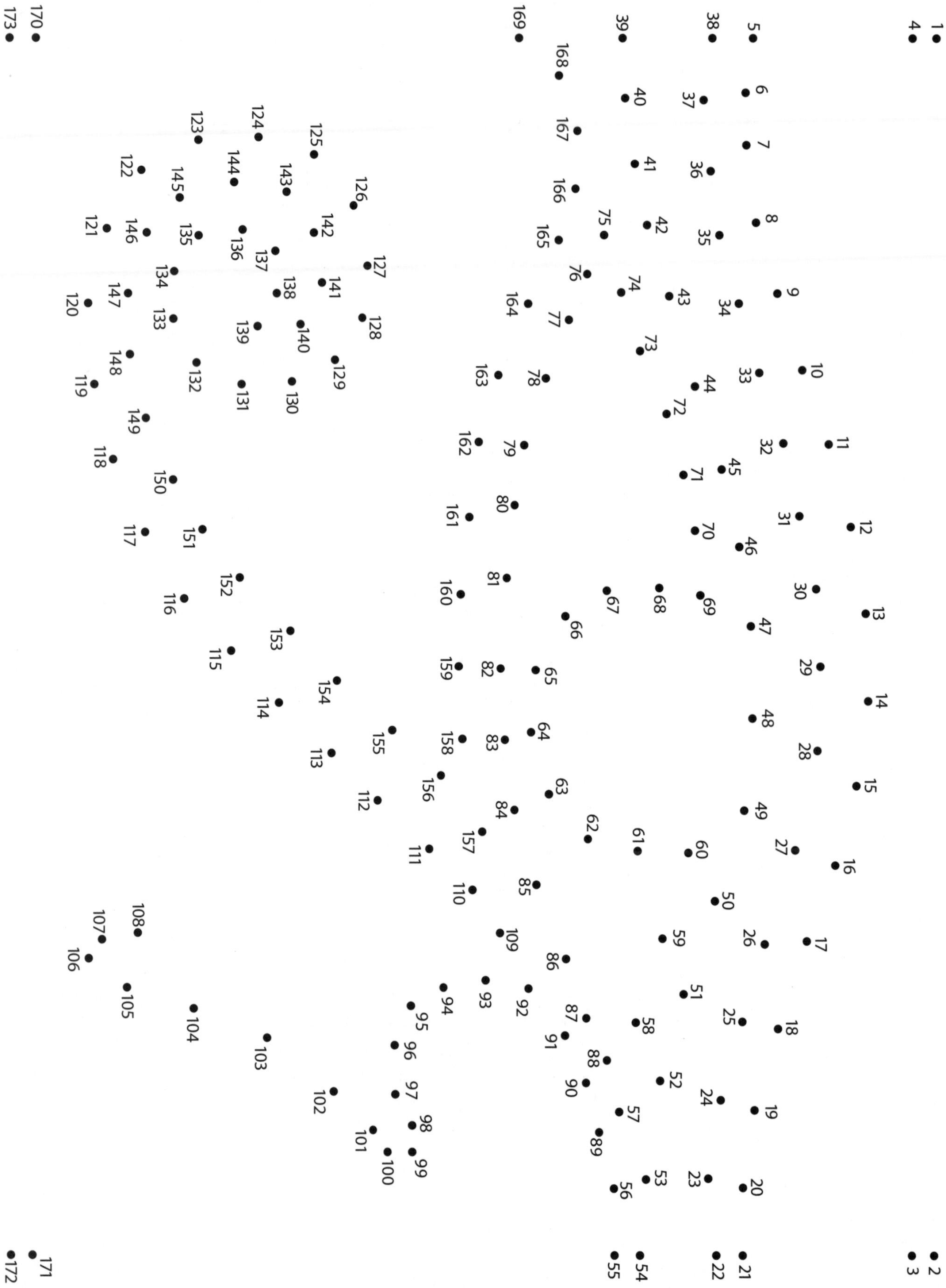

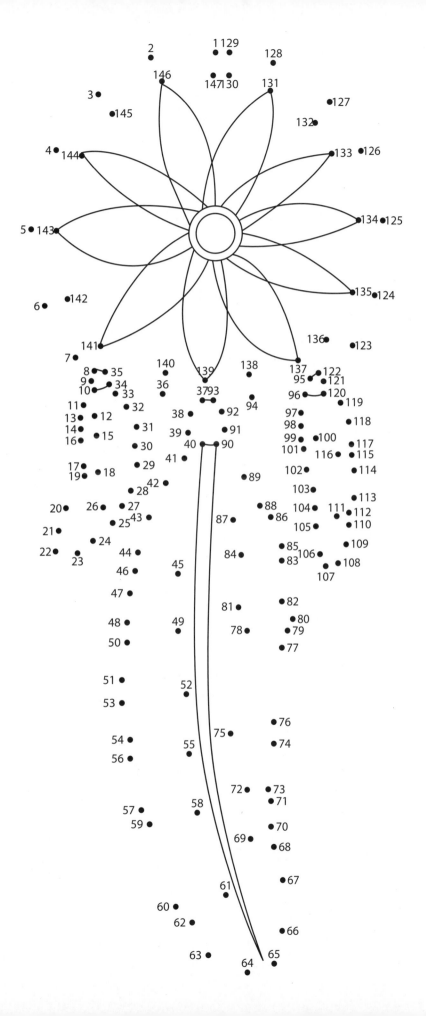

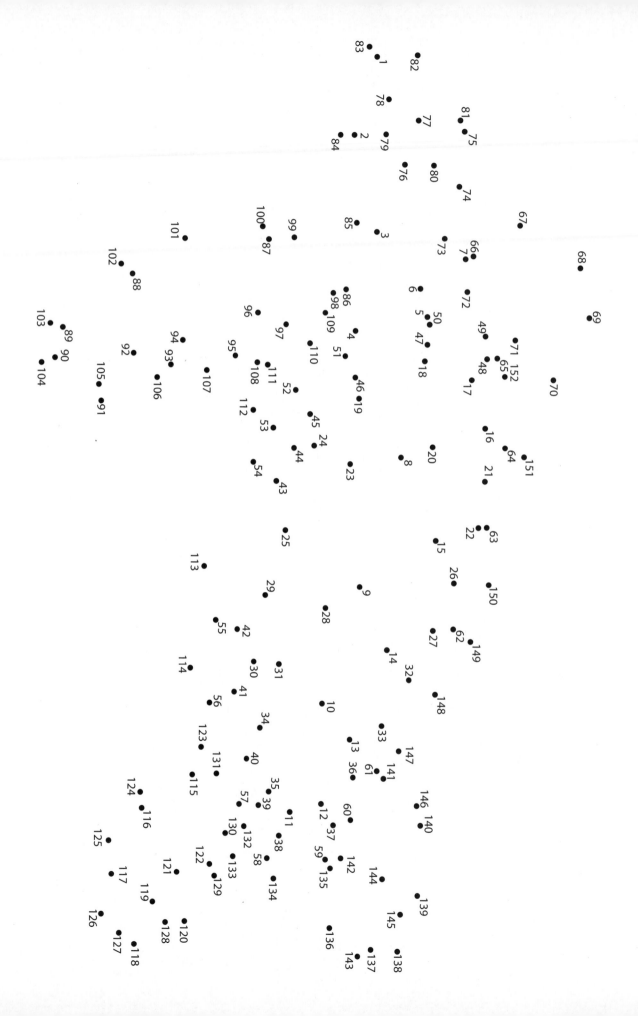

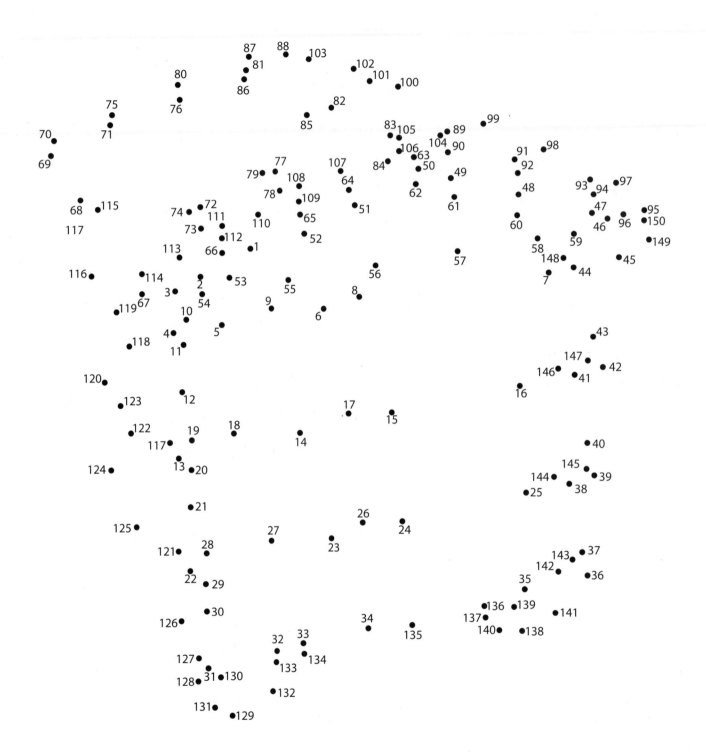

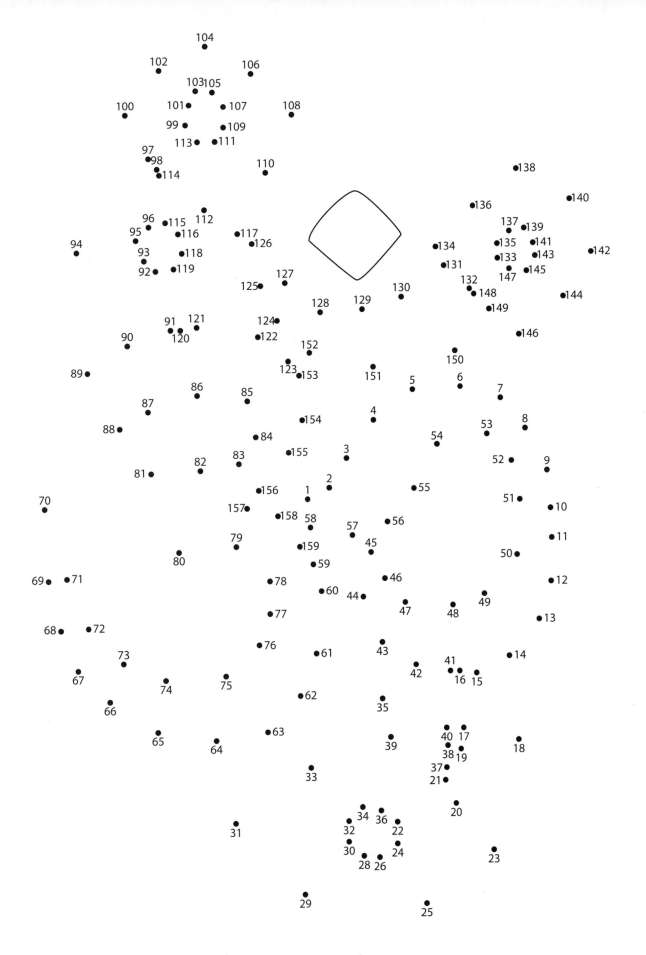

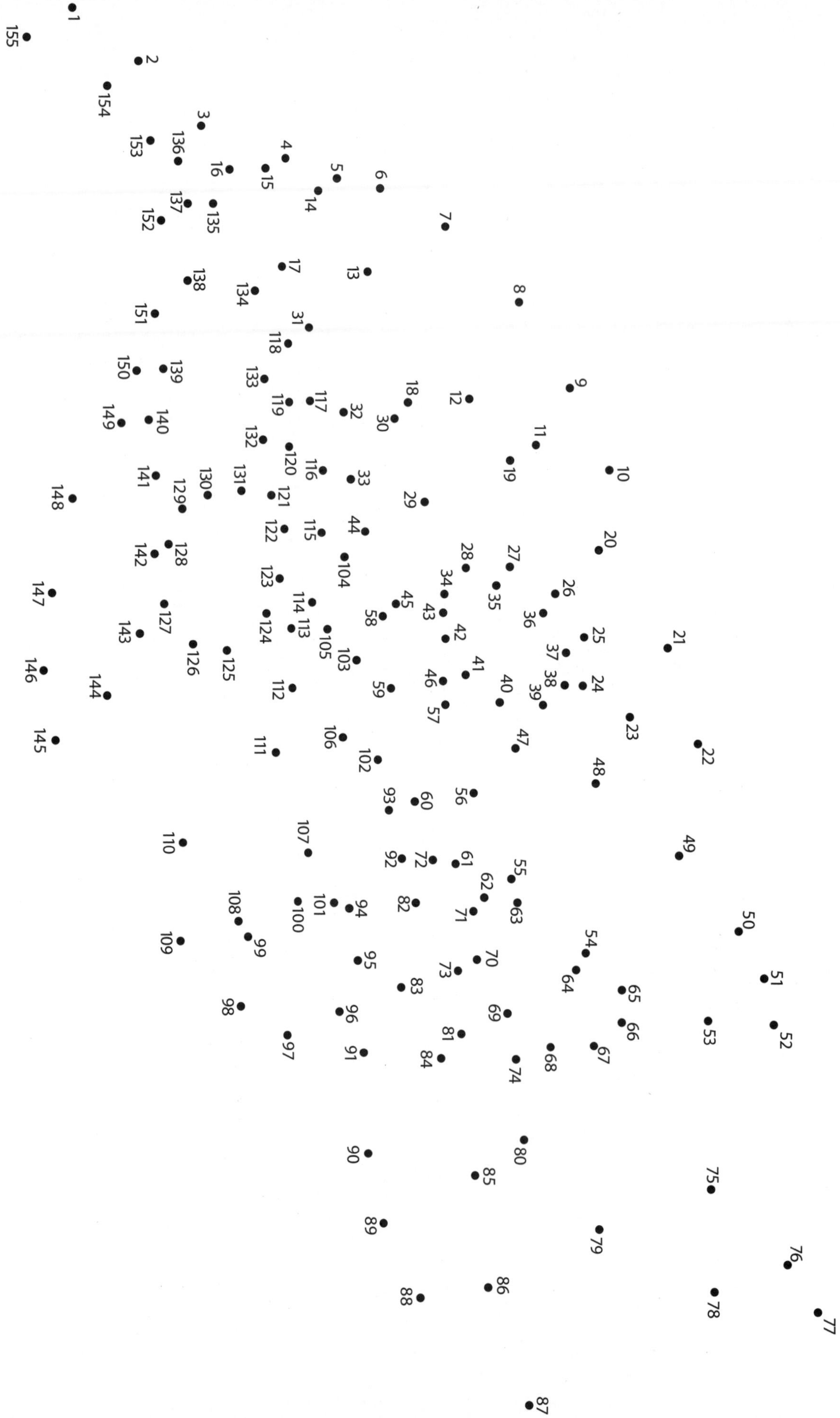

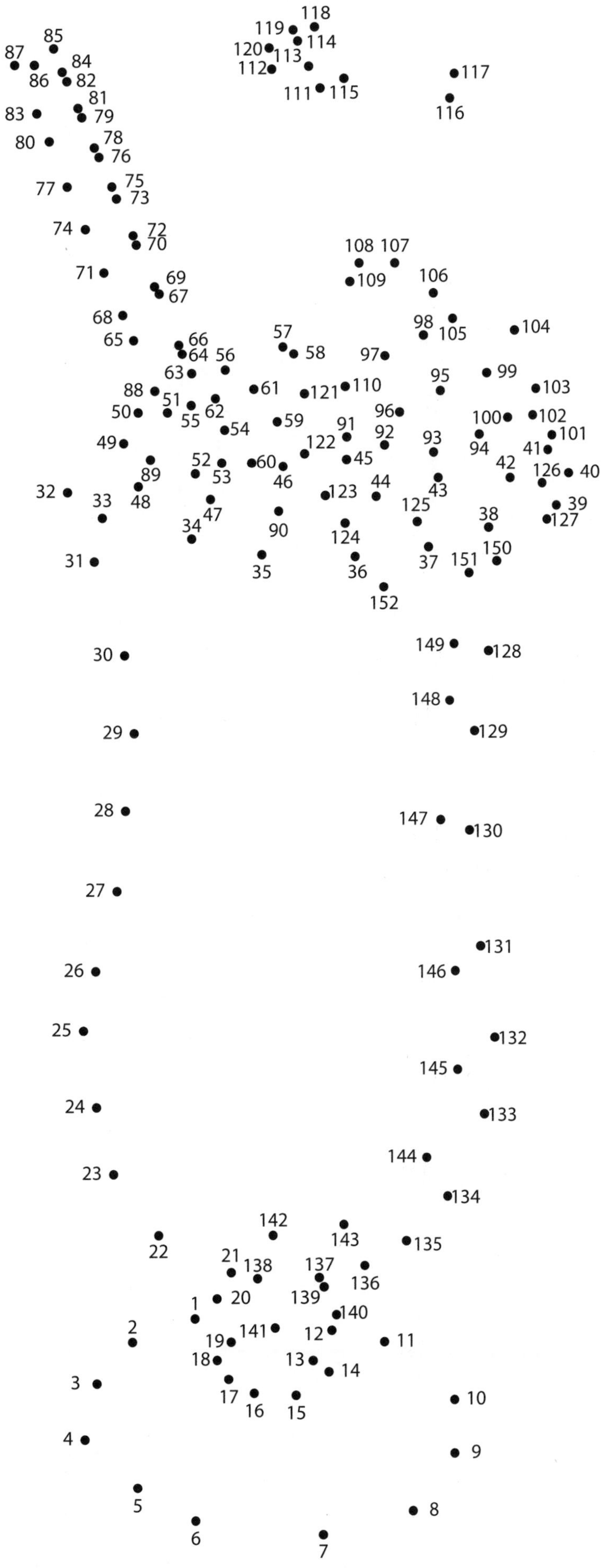

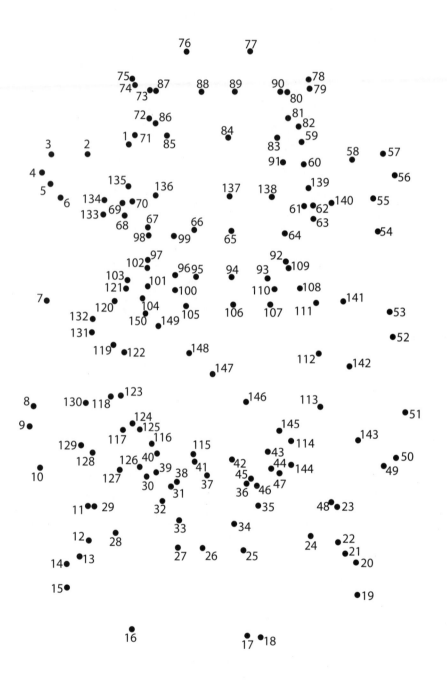

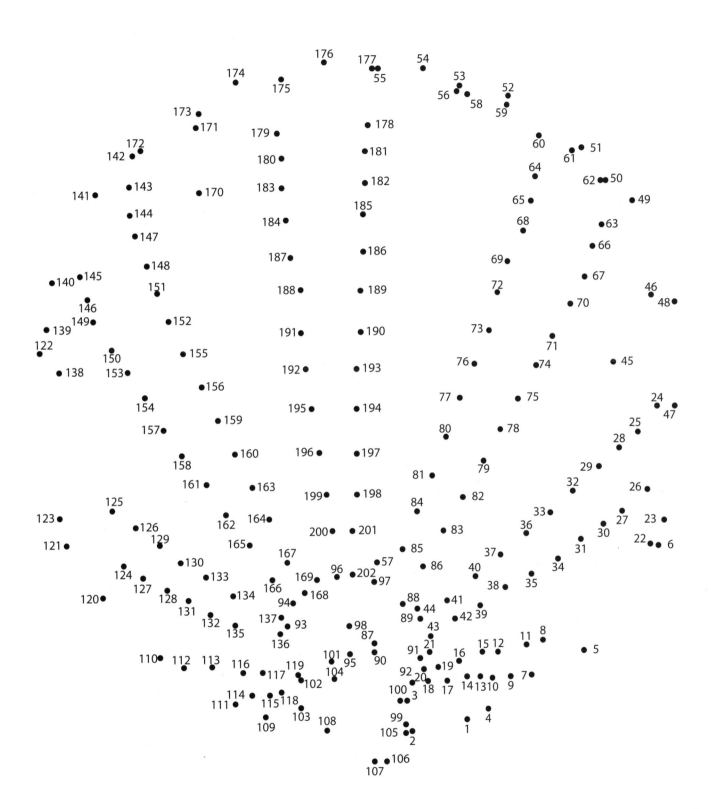

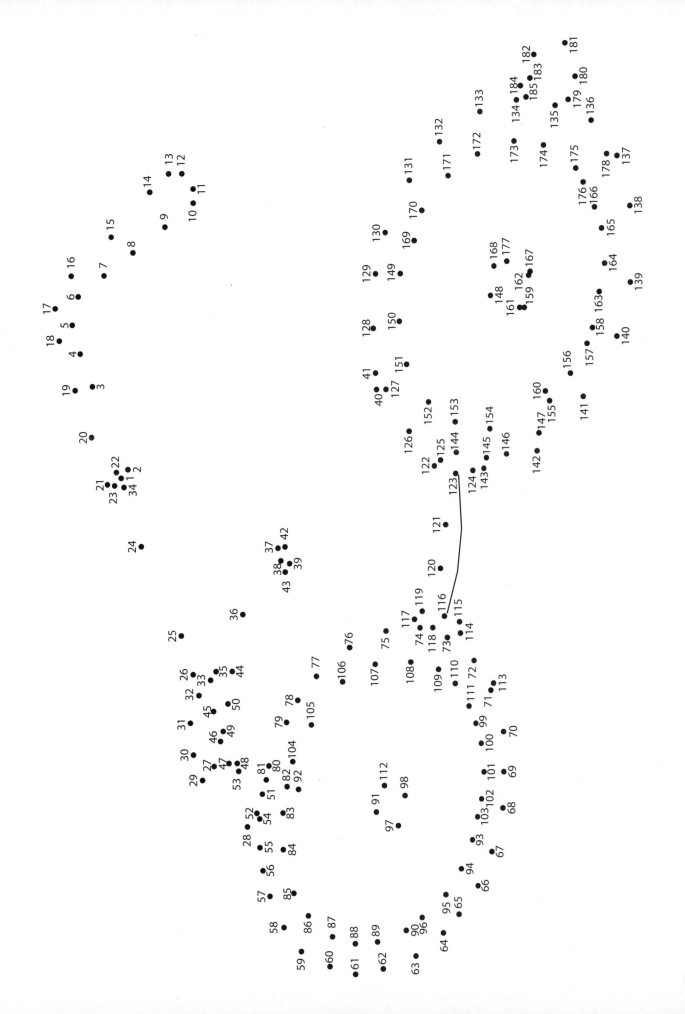

232

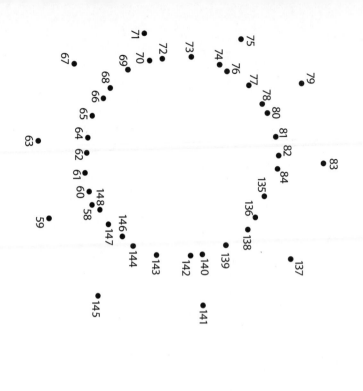

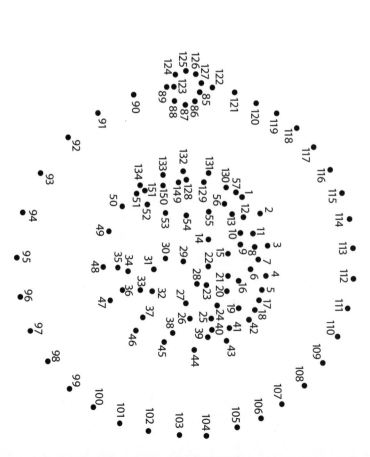

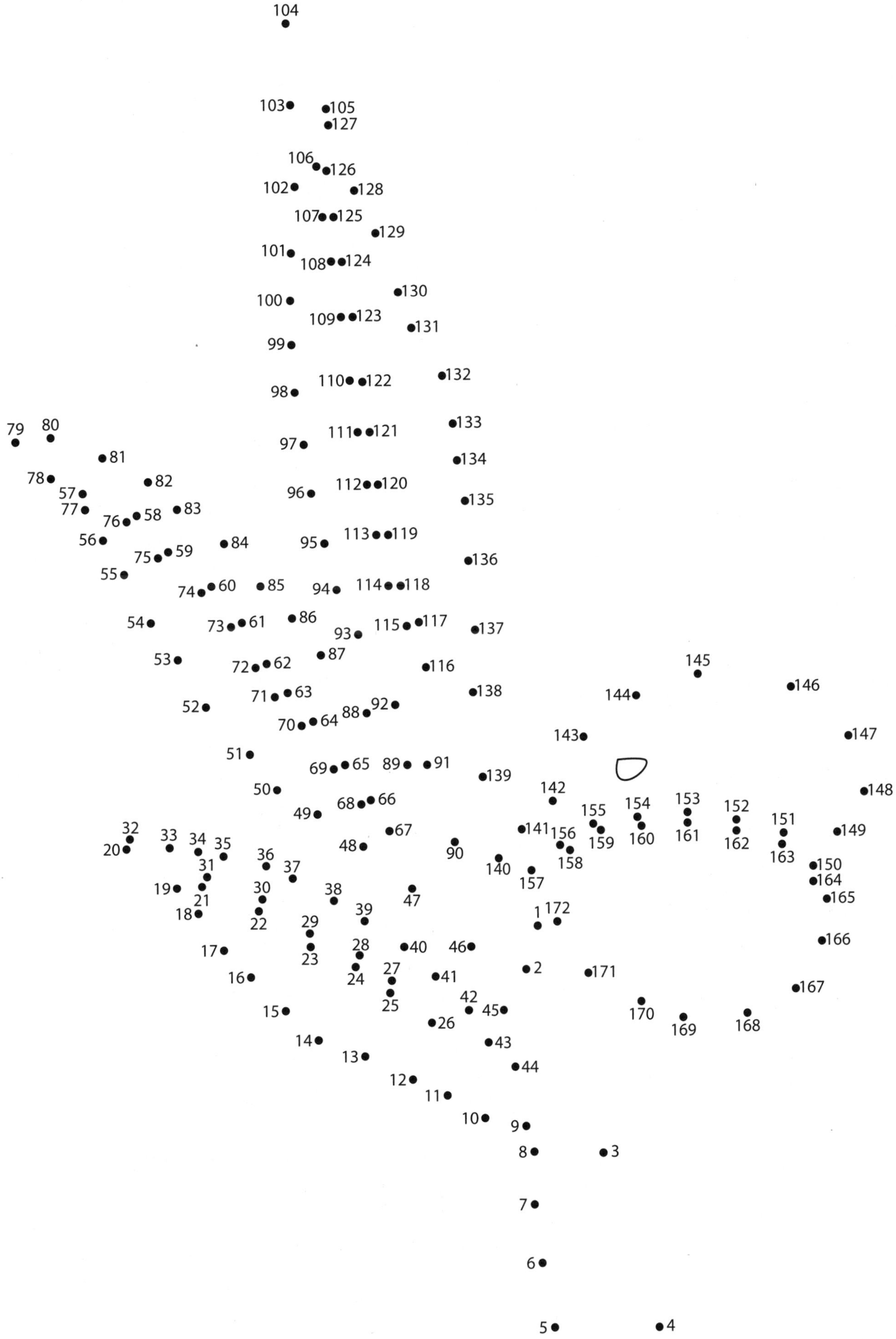

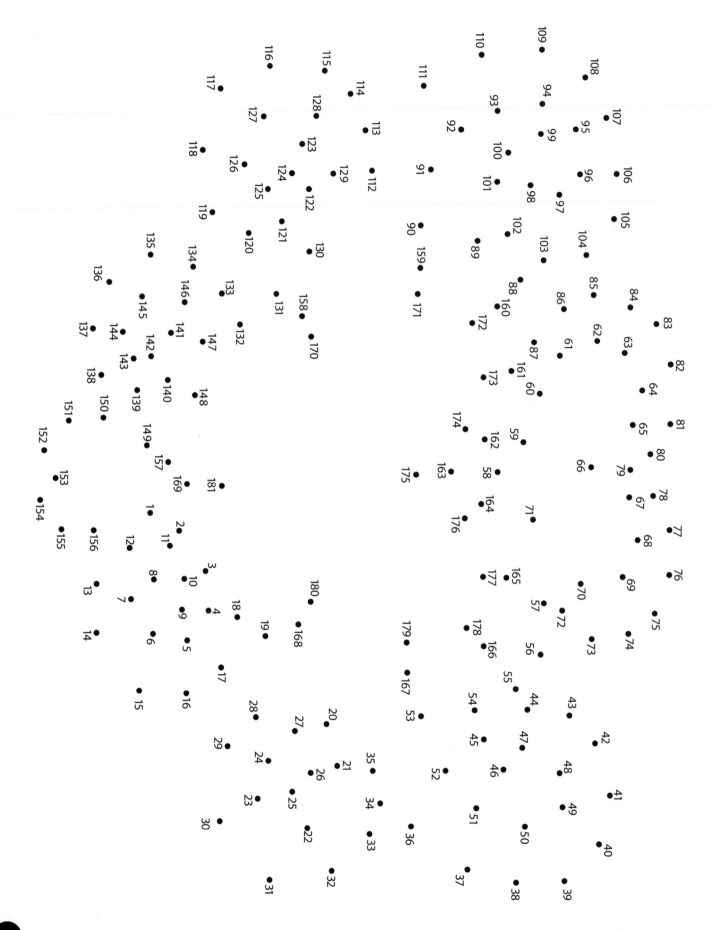

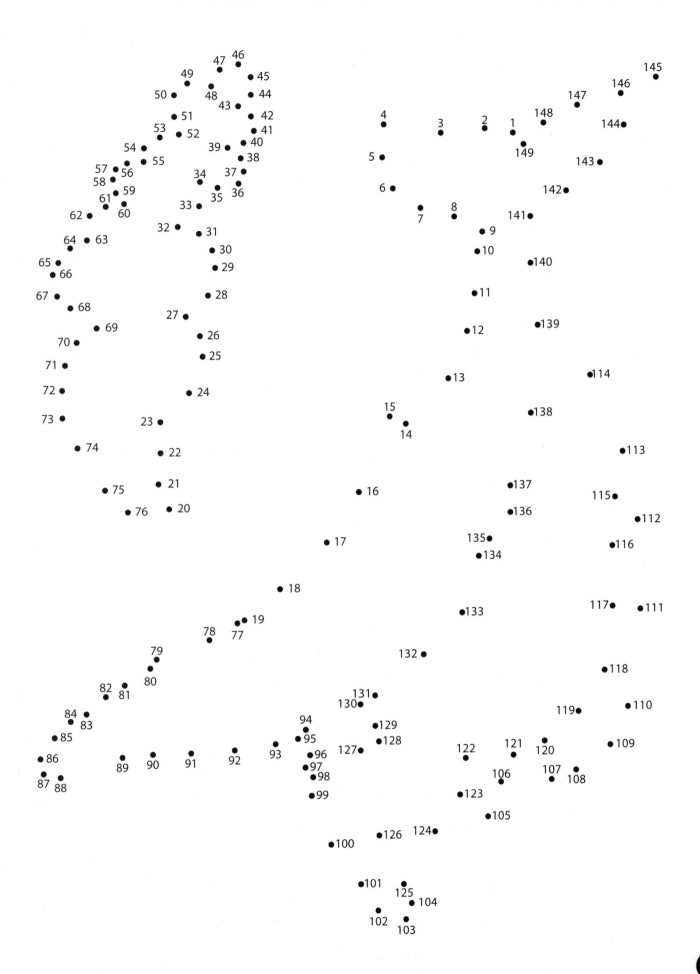

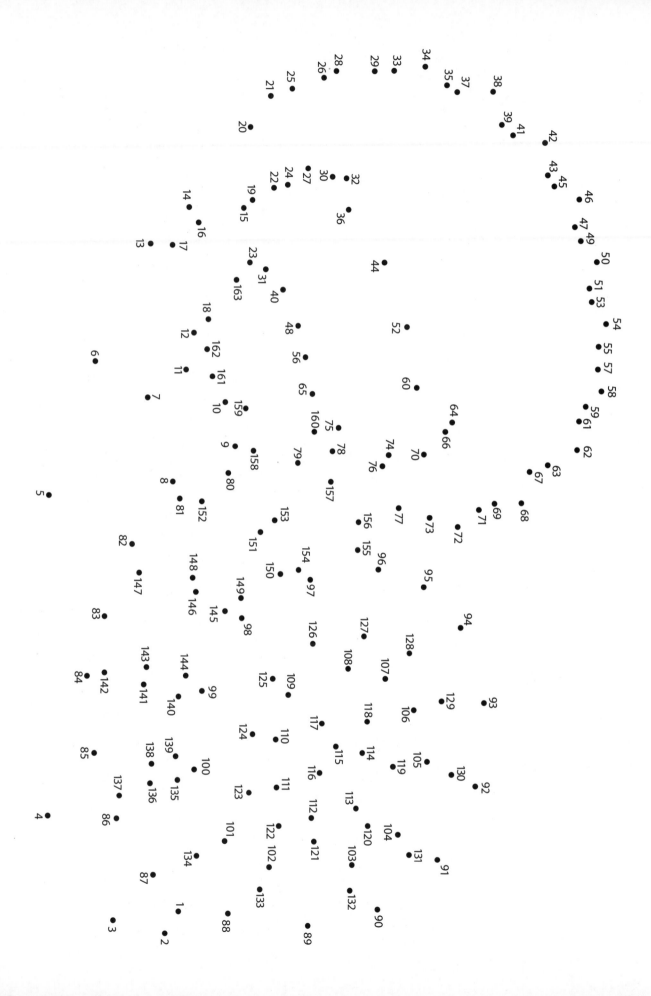

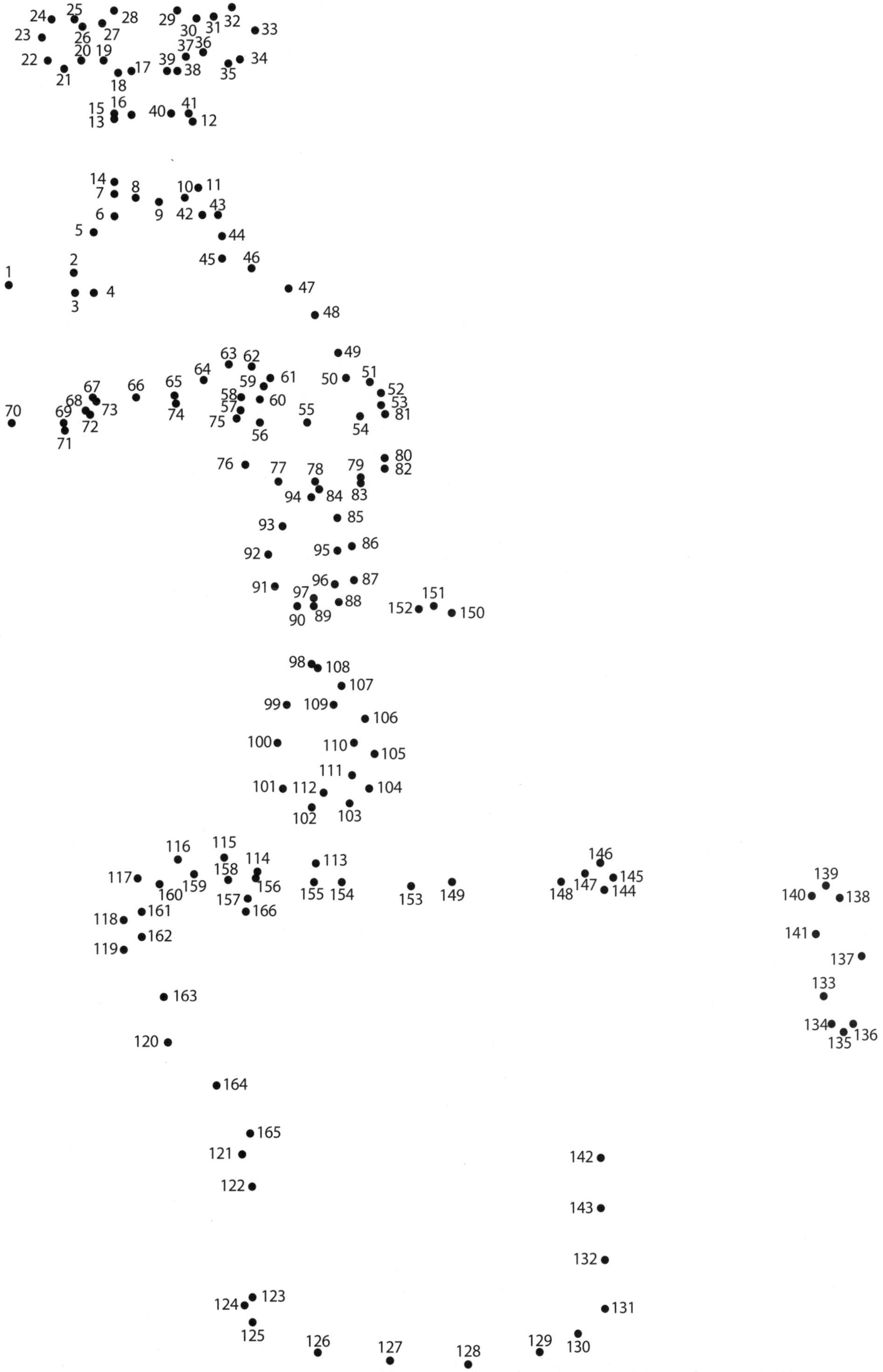

A dot-to-dot puzzle with numbered dots from 1 to 166.

24 • 25 • 28 • 29 • 31 32
23 • 26 27 30 • 33
22 • 20 19 37 36 • 34
21 17 39 38 35
18
15 16 40 • 41
13 12

14 • 8 10 • 11
7 • 43
6 • 9 42
5
2 44
1 45 • 46
3 • 4 47
48
63 62 • 49
64 59 • 61 50 • 51
66 65 58 • 52
68 67 60 53
70 69 73 74 57 55 81
72 75 56 54
71
80
76 77 78 79 82
94 84 83
93 85
92 95 86
91 96 87
97 88
90 89 152 • 151 • 150

98 • 108
107
99 • 109
106
100 • 110 105
111
101 112 104
102 103

116 115
117 158 114 113 146
160 159 156 145
157 155 154 153 149 148 147 144
118 161 166
119 162 139
140 • 138
141
163 137
120 133
134 136
135

164

165
121 142
122 143
132
124 123 131
125 126 127 128 129 130

241

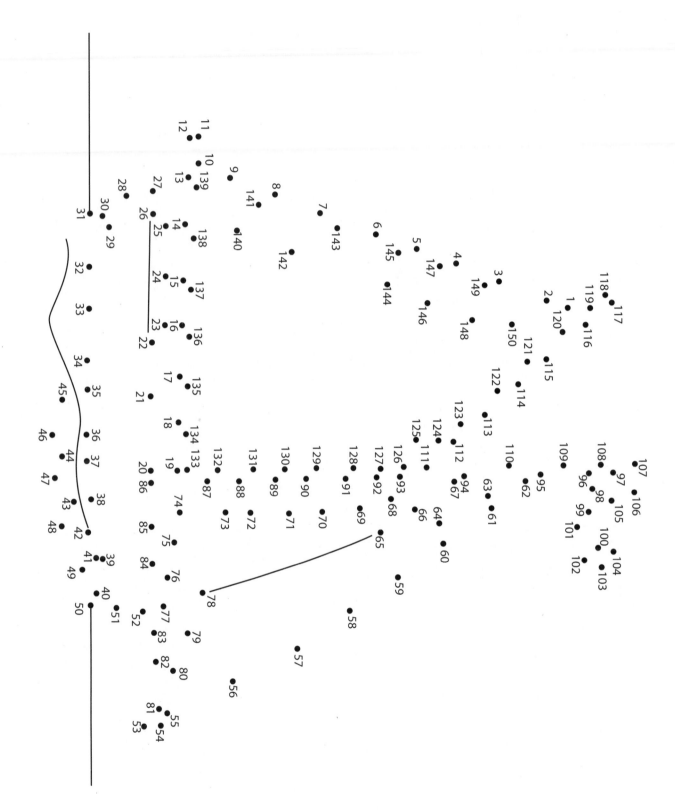

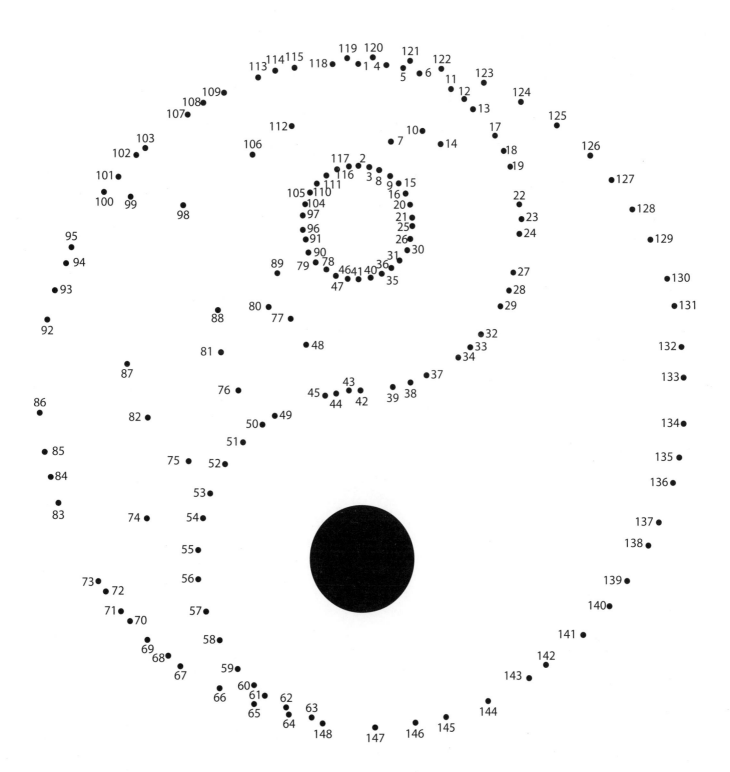

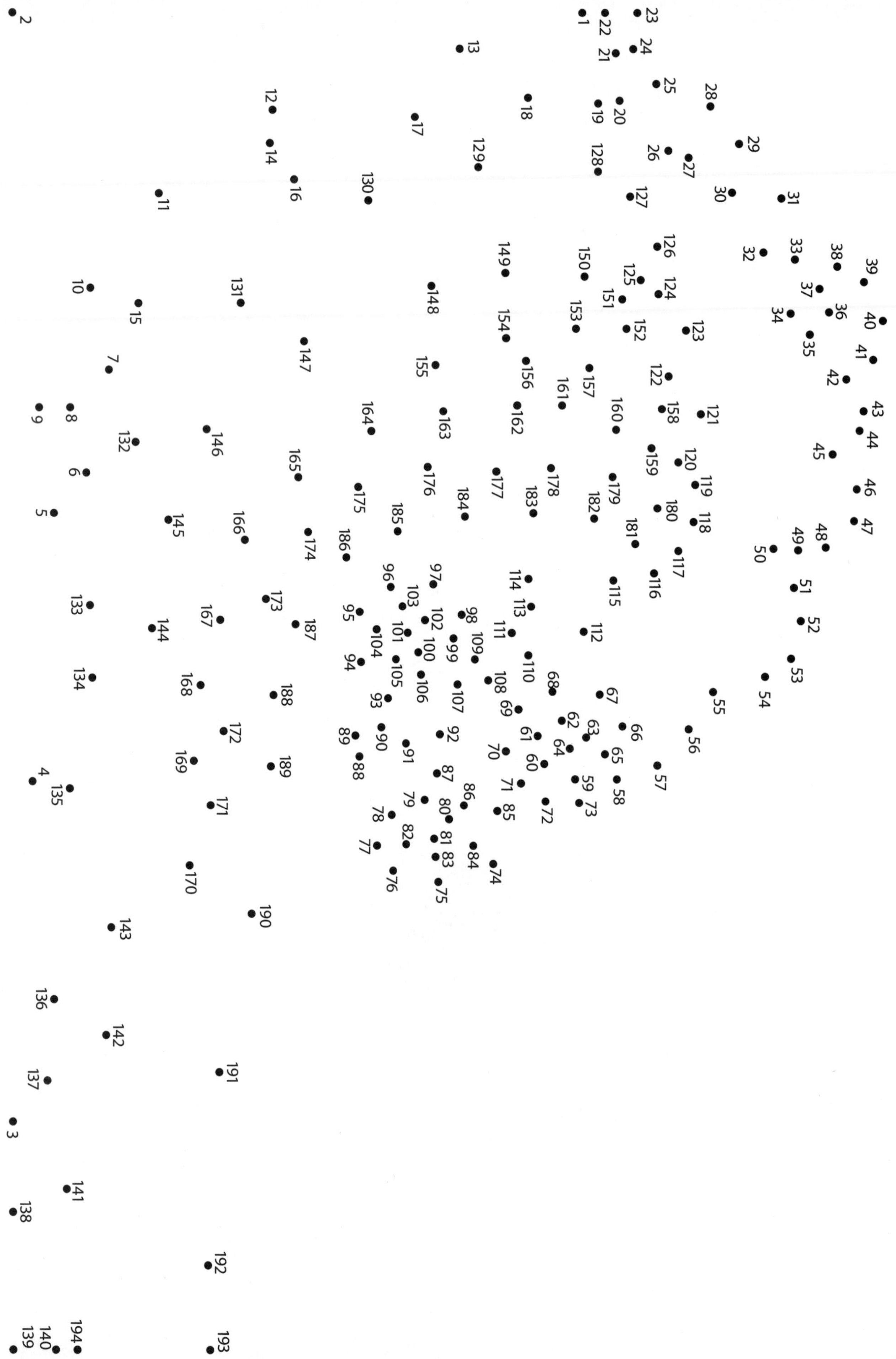

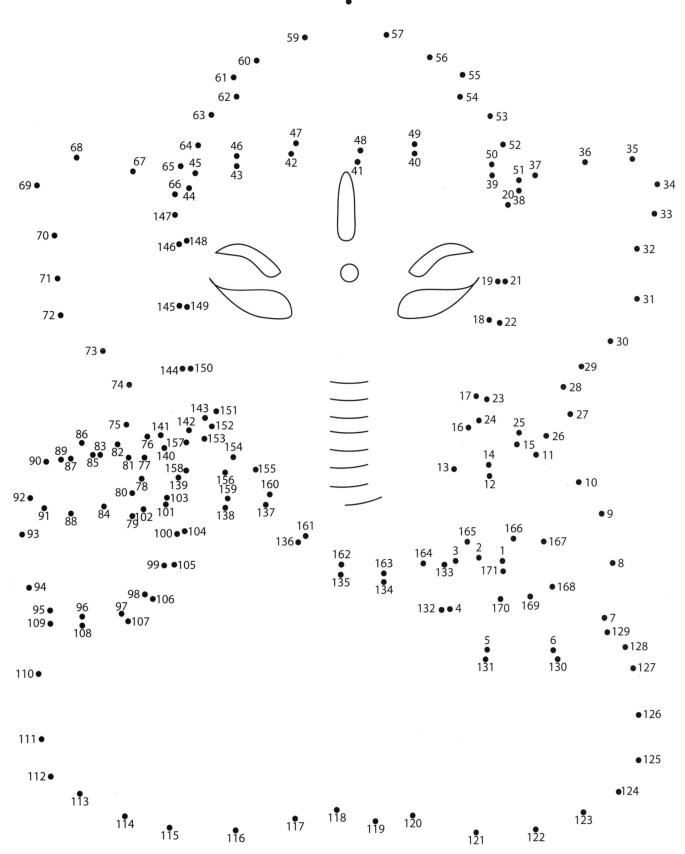

245

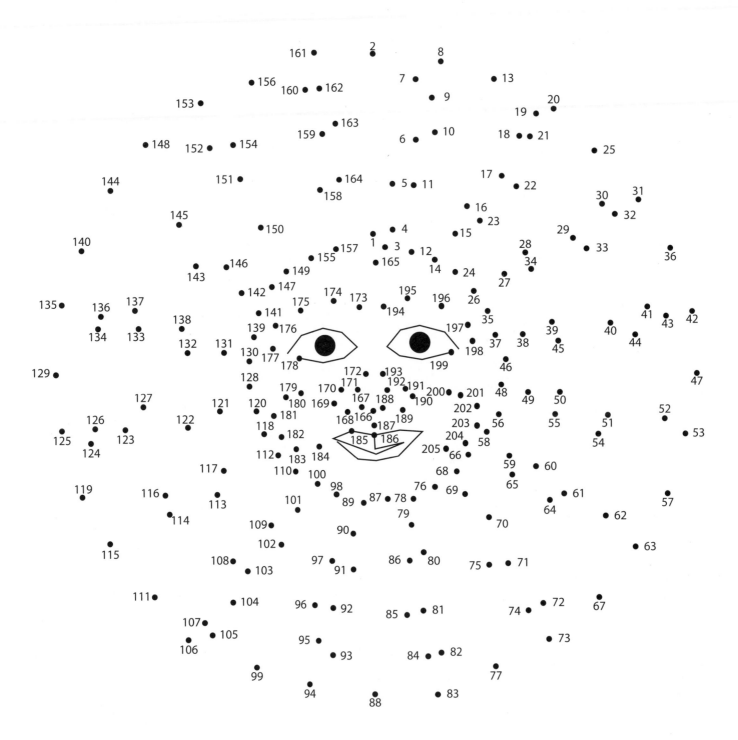

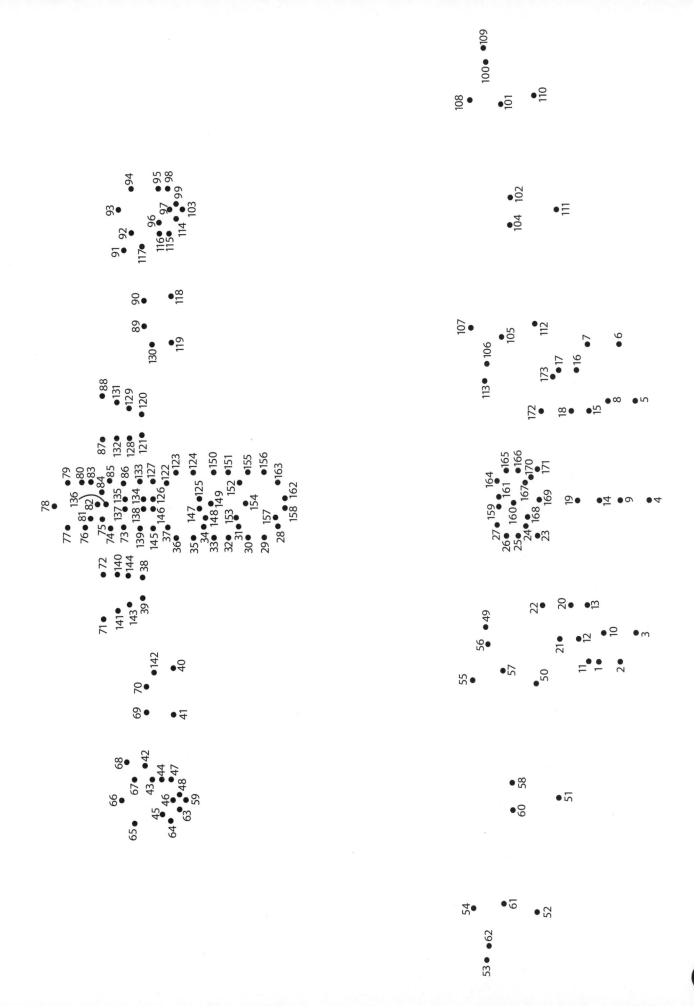

143

142 144

141 145

140

146

139

138 147

137

136 148

149 158

135 150

151 114

134

152

132 111 112 113
133 153 154
110 109 108
131 130 156 155 115
157 98 99
116 117 106 107
119 118 105 104
129 120
121 122 123 100 101 102 103 159
128 126 125 124 95 94 93 92
97 96
91
127 2 85 86 87 88 89 90 160
1 3 81 80
4 84 83 31 63 82 64 79
5 78
6 7 8 61 62 74 75 77
73 72 76
11 10 9 32 60 59 71
29 70
12 57 58 69
13 14 65 66 67 68
16 15 56 55 52 51 50 49
33
17 28
54 48
18 19 20 43 44 45 53 47
22 21 41 40 46
23 27 34 42 39
38
24 37
25 26 35 36 248

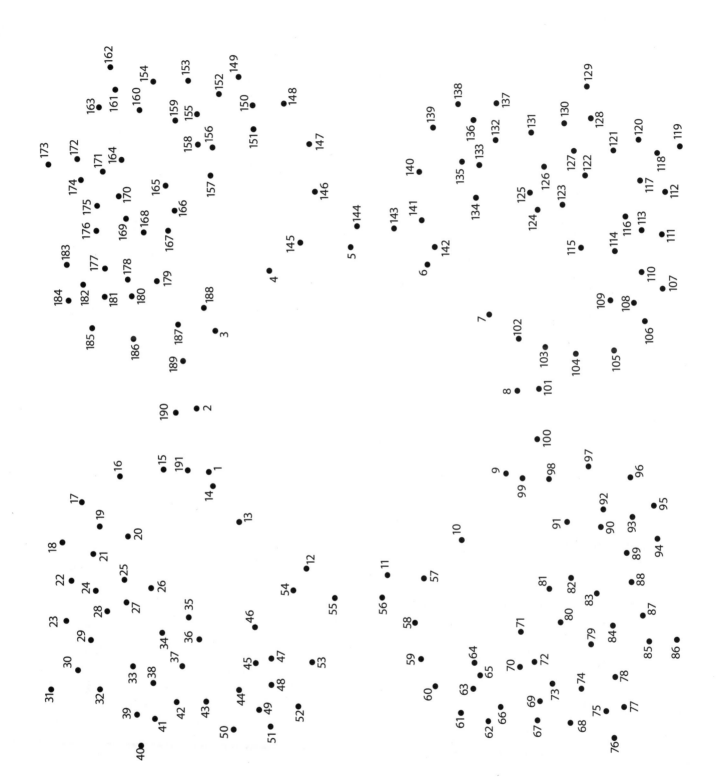

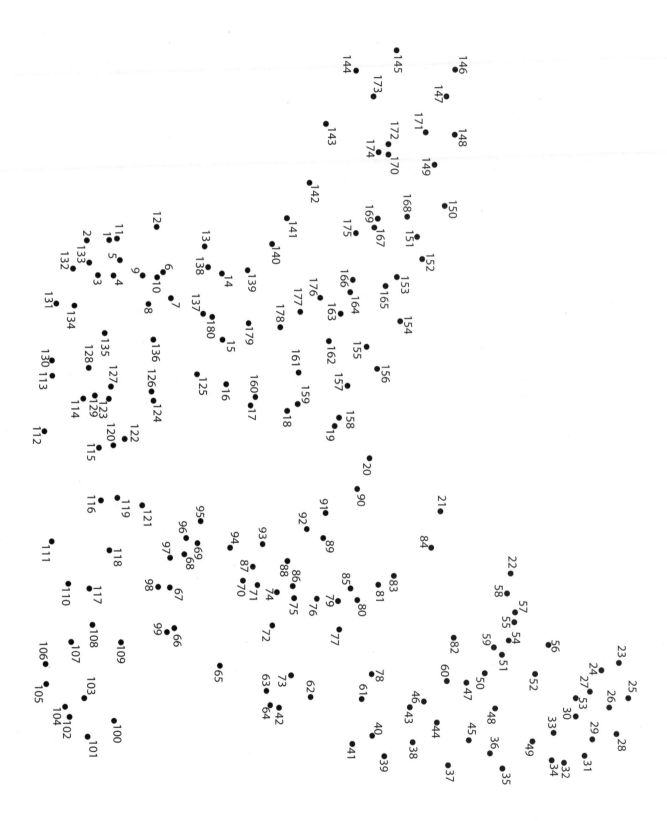

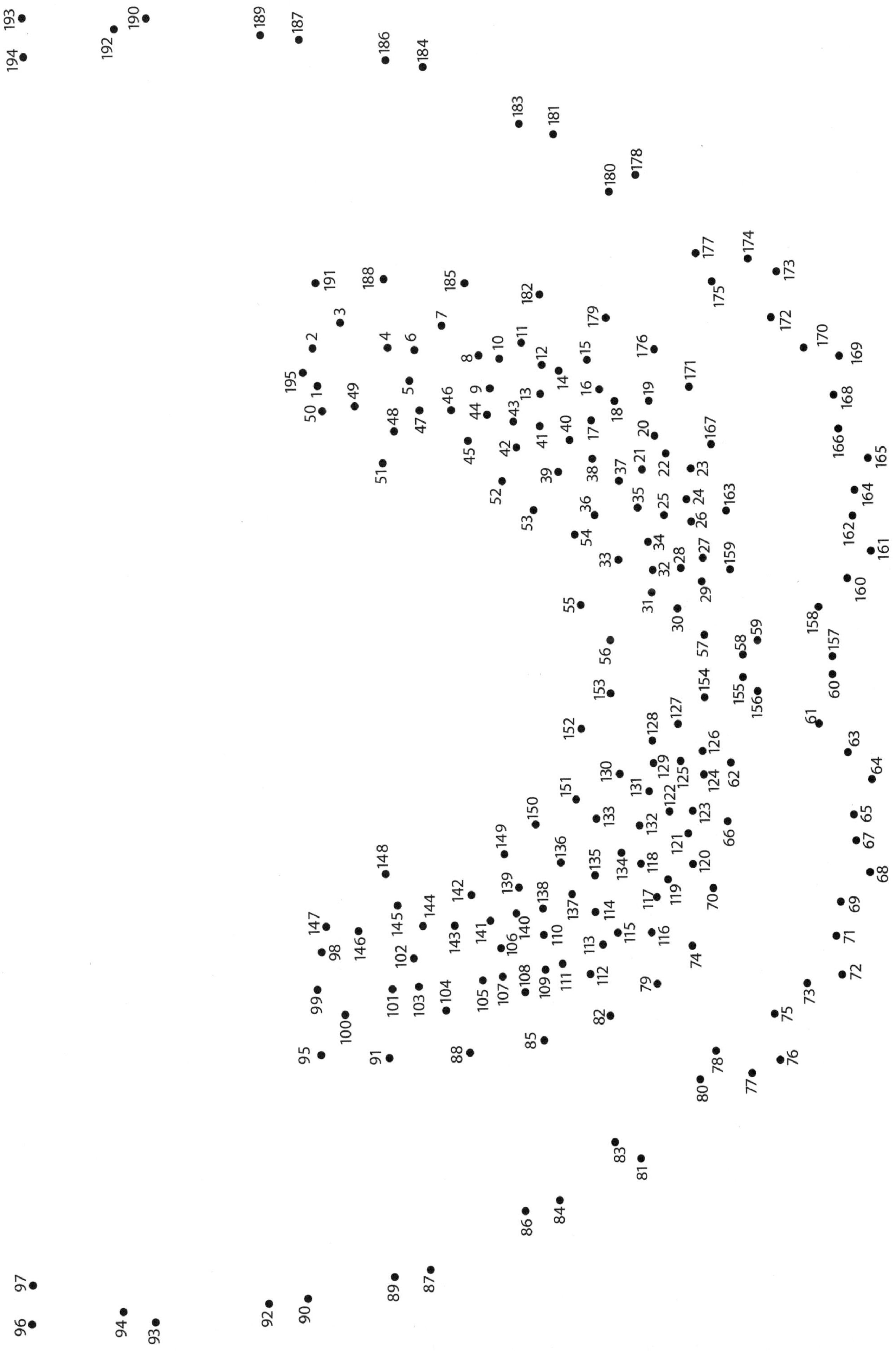

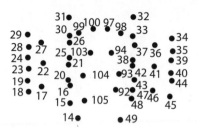

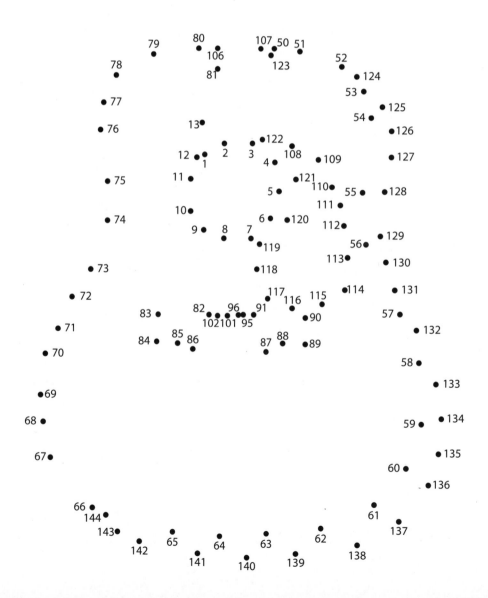

List of Illustrations